Java

by Building Mini Apps

by
STEMSCHOOL

Master Java by Building Mini-Apps

Learn Java the Practical Way with Real Projects

By

STEM School

This Page Left Intentionally Blank

Contents

Chapter 1

Introduction to Java & Project-Based Learning

Java, first released by Sun Microsystems in 1995 and now maintained by Oracle, remains one of the most widely used and enduring programming languages in the world. Its design principle of "write once, run anywhere" made it a go-to choice for developers who needed platform independence, and this strength still holds today.

Java is at the heart of a wide array of applications. In desktop software, it powers sophisticated applications such as integrated development environments (like IntelliJ IDEA), graphical tools, and business enterprise software. When it comes to mobile development, Java serves as the foundation for Android applications, which dominate the global smartphone market. In the world of embedded systems, Java also plays a strong role. With Java ME (Micro Edition), it supports smart cards, set-top boxes, and embedded IoT devices. Its scalability and reliability make it suitable for everything from hobbyist-level tools to enterprise-grade platforms.

Moreover, Java's mature ecosystem, vast libraries, and robust documentation make it a perfect language for both beginners and professionals. Learning Java not only equips you with a powerful programming language but also provides insight into the software development lifecycle, object-oriented programming, and the design patterns that underlie most modern applications.

Why Learning Java Through Projects ?

Traditional learning methods focus on syntax, theoretical concepts, and rote exercises, which often fail to bridge the gap between theory and real-world application. In contrast, learning Java through hands-on projects accelerates skill development. This approach ensures that you internalize core programming concepts because you're applying them in context.

When you build mini-applications such as calculators, to-do list managers, game engines, or chatbots, you tackle real challenges such as debugging, problem-solving, user interaction, and logical thinking. These experiences mirror the problems faced by professional developers and prepare you to work confidently in production environments.

By the end of this book, you will have built several Java projects from scratch. Each project is designed not only to demonstrate a specific concept (such as loops, file I/O, or object-oriented design) but also to culminate in a useful, working product that you can run, customize, and share.

Setting Up Your Java Development Environment

Before diving into code, it's crucial to set up a proper Java development environment. This environment will allow you to write, compile, debug, and run your Java programs efficiently.

The core component of your development environment is the **Java Development Kit (JDK)**. The JDK contains the Java compiler (`javac`), Java Runtime Environment (JRE), and other tools required for building Java programs.

You'll also need an **Integrated Development Environment (IDE)**, which offers features like syntax highlighting, auto-completion, and real-time debugging. Two of the most popular Java IDEs are **IntelliJ IDEA** and **Eclipse**. IntelliJ IDEA is known for its sleek interface, intelligent code completion, and developer-friendly environment. Eclipse is widely used in the industry and offers extensive plugin support.

In addition, modern Java development often utilizes **build automation tools** like **Maven** and **Gradle**. These tools help manage project dependencies, compile code, run tests, and package applications.

The following table provides a comparison of these tools and environments

Tool	Description	Use Case
JDK (Java SE)	Core Java tools and compiler	Required for all Java programming tasks
IntelliJ IDEA	Advanced IDE with smart features and debugging tools	Ideal for beginners and advanced developers
Eclipse	Open-source IDE with extensive plugin support	Preferred in academic and enterprise environments
Maven	Build tool with XML-based configuration	Used for dependency and project management
Gradle	Build tool with script-based (Groovy/Kotlin) configuration	Modern alternative to Maven

After installation, you should verify your setup by opening a terminal or command prompt and typing

```
java -version
javac -version
```

Both commands should output the installed versions, confirming that your system is ready.

Your First Java Program Hello World Walkthrough

Let us now write our very first Java program. The famous "Hello World" example demonstrates the structure of a basic Java application.

Open your IDE (e.g., IntelliJ) and create a new Java project named `HelloWorld`. Inside the project, create a new Java class called `HelloWorld`.

Here's the code

```
public class HelloWorld {
    public static void main(String[] args) {
        System.out.println("Hello, World!");
    }
}
```

Let's break this down

- `public class HelloWorld` defines a new class. In Java, every program must be part of a class.

- `public static void main(String[] args)` is the entry point of the program. This is where execution begins.
- `System.out.println("Hello, World!");` prints text to the console.

Click the "Run" button or use the terminal to compile and run the program

```
javac HelloWorld.java
java HelloWorld
```

You should see `Hello, World!`

Preview of Your First Hands-On Java Project

Let's preview the first mini-project we'll build in the next chapter a **Simple Command-Line Calculator**.

This calculator will

- Accept user input from the terminal.
- Support basic operations like addition, subtraction, multiplication, and division.
- Handle invalid input gracefully.
- Be structured using Java classes and methods.

Here's a conceptual diagram of how the calculator project will be organized

This project will teach you how to

- Use `Scanner` for input
- Parse user input
- Use conditionals and loops
- Structure code into reusable methods

It may seem simple, but this first project lays the groundwork for more complex ones that follow. Each future project will build on these concepts, introducing GUIs, file handling, APIs, and multithreading, step-by-step.

By the end of this chapter, you've gained a high-level understanding of Java's role in the world of software development and the immense value of project-based learning. You've also set up a complete Java development environment, written your first program, and previewed an upcoming hands-on project.

In the next chapter, we'll start building your first Java mini-application from scratch. Every line of code will be explained in detail so you not only understand **how** to build, but also **why** it works. This project-based journey will gradually elevate your skills from beginner to confident Java developer.

Let's start building!

Chapter 2

Java Fundamentals through a Calculator App

Understanding a programming language like Java begins with mastering its fundamental building blocks. These fundamentals include variables, data types, operators, and control structures. In this chapter, we will dive deep into these concepts by creating a hands-on, functional command-line calculator application. Instead of studying theory in isolation, we will build our knowledge as we write real code that takes input from users, performs calculations, and returns results — just like professional developers do in the real world.

The command-line calculator is more than just a beginner project. It represents the perfect vehicle to explore core Java programming logic while interacting with actual users via a console. As we work on the calculator, you will learn how to store values in memory (variables), understand the different types of data Java works with (data types), use Java's built-in arithmetic (operators), and make decisions in code using conditionals and loops (control structures). You will also learn how to handle errors, read input from users, and debug your program to identify and fix issues. By the end of this chapter, you'll have a practical tool that you coded entirely yourself — a rewarding milestone in your Java learning journey.

Understanding Variables, Data Types, and Operators

At the heart of any Java application are **variables**. These are memory containers that hold data. A variable in Java must be declared with a **data type**, which defines the kind of value it can store. Java is a **strongly typed language**, meaning you must define the type of each variable before using it.

The basic syntax for declaring a variable looks like this

```
int number = 5;
```

Here, `int` is the data type, `number` is the variable name, and `5` is the value assigned to it.

Java offers a wide range of data types, categorized as **primitive** and **non-primitive** types. Let's look at a comparison of commonly used primitive data types in Java

Data Type	Size	Description	Example Value
int	4 bytes	Integer numbers	10
double	8	Decimal numbers	10.5

Data Type	Size	Description	Example Value
	bytes		
char	2 bytes	Single character	'A'
boolean	1 bit	True or false value	true
long	8 bytes	Larger integers	100000000L
float	4 bytes	Decimal with less precision	3.14f

Each data type allows you to store specific kinds of values and ensures memory efficiency and performance. Choosing the right type is essential for writing optimized applications.

Java also provides **operators**, which allow you to perform computations and comparisons. The most common operators include

Category	Operators	Description
Arithmetic	+, -, *, /, %	Add, subtract, multiply, divide, modulo
Relational	==, !=, >, <	Equality, inequality, greater than, etc.
Logical	&&, ||, !	Logical AND, OR, NOT
Assignment	=, +=, -=, *=	Assign and update values

Using these building blocks, we can start constructing logic for our calculator.

Making Decisions and Repeating Actions

Control structures are essential to direct the flow of your application. They allow you to make decisions (e.g., using `if` or `switch`) and repeat actions (e.g., using `while` or `for` loops). Let's explore these through examples relevant to our calculator.

The `if-else` structure lets your program choose between different options based on conditions

```
if (operator.equals("+")) {
    result = num1 + num2;
} else if (operator.equals("-")) {
    result = num1 - num2;
}
```

The `switch` statement provides a cleaner way to handle multiple options

```
switch (operator) {
    case "+"
        result = num1 + num2;
        break;
    case "-"
        result = num1 - num2;
        break;
    default
        System.out.println("Unsupported operation");
}
```

To repeat actions — for instance, to keep asking the user for input until they want to quit — we use loops

```
while (true) {
    // Prompt for input and perform calculation
    // Break the loop if the user types 'exit'
}
```

The following diagram illustrates a typical control flow for our calculator

20

```
Start Calculator
```

```
Show Menu
```

```
Read Input Numbers
```

```
Perform Operation
```

```
Display Result
```

```
Ask to Continue?
```

Hands-On Project Building the CLI Calculator

Now, let's build the actual calculator app. Open your IDE and create a new Java class named CalculatorApp.

Here is the complete source code, with commentary

```java
import java.util.Scanner;
```

```java
public class CalculatorApp {
    public static void main(String[] args) {
        Scanner scanner = new Scanner(System.in);
        boolean continueCalculation = true;

        System.out.println("Welcome to the CLI
Calculator!");

        while (continueCalculation) {
            System.out.print("Enter first number  ");
            double num1 = scanner.nextDouble();

            System.out.print("Enter operator (+, -,
*, /)  ");
            String operator = scanner.next();

            System.out.print("Enter second number
");
            double num2 = scanner.nextDouble();

            double result;

            switch (operator) {
                case "+"
                    result = num1 + num2;
                    break;
                case "-"
                    result = num1 - num2;
                    break;
                case "*"
                    result = num1 * num2;
                    break;
                case "/"
                    if (num2 != 0) {
                        result = num1 / num2;
                    } else {
                        System.out.println("Error
Division by zero is not allowed.");
                        continue;
```

```
                    }
                    break;
                default
                    System.out.println("Invalid
operator.");

                    continue;
            }

            System.out.println("Result   " + result);

            System.out.print("Do you want to perform
another calculation? (yes/no)   ");
            String response = scanner.next();

            if (!response.equalsIgnoreCase("yes")) {
                continueCalculation = false;
            }
        }

        System.out.println("Thank you for using the
calculator.");
        scanner.close();
    }
}
```

This project helps you understand user input handling, switch-case control flow, loops, and data type operations — all in one cohesive program.

Debugging Techniques and Input Handling

As you build and test the calculator, you may encounter unexpected results or crashes. Learning to debug is a crucial skill. In Java, debugging can be done using IDE features or simple print statements.

For example, if your division is producing incorrect results, you can print out the values of the operands before the operation

```
System.out.println("Debug  num1 = " + num1 + ", num2
= " + num2);
```

Also, when handling input, it's essential to anticipate and handle errors. For instance, if a user types a letter instead of a number, the program might crash. To handle this, wrap input reading in a try-catch block

```
try {
    double num = scanner.nextDouble();
} catch (InputMismatchException e) {
    System.out.println("Invalid input. Please enter a
number.");
    scanner.next(); // clear the invalid input
}
```

Robust programs must always validate and sanitize input. This ensures stability and a smooth user experience, especially when scaling applications later.

Summary Building Skills Through Projects

This chapter not only introduced essential Java programming concepts but also tied them to a working CLI calculator project that you can now run, modify, and expand. You've learned about variables, data types, and operators and how to apply them within control structures like if-else, switch, and loops.

You've also begun practicing how to read user input, validate it, and debug your code for correctness.

The calculator project is an excellent foundation for further learning. In future chapters, we will enhance this simple tool into more advanced versions — including graphical user interfaces (GUIs), memory functionality, history tracking, and even scientific calculations — while continuing to introduce new Java concepts and development skills.

By building, testing, and improving real applications like this one, you're not just learning Java — you're becoming a Java developer.

In the next chapter, we will explore **Object-Oriented Programming (OOP)** and begin refactoring our calculator to use classes and objects effectively. The journey continues — and your skills will grow with each project.

Chapter 3

Object-Oriented Programming with a Library Management System

After learning the foundational syntax and control flow of Java through a command-line calculator, it is time to move into the heart of Java — **Object-Oriented Programming (OOP)**. Java is fundamentally an object-oriented language. To become proficient in Java and build large, maintainable, and modular applications, you must understand and master the core principles of OOP. These principles not only shape how Java applications are written but also dictate how software is structured across the industry — whether you're building games, banking software, or inventory systems.

This chapter will help you dive deeply into the most crucial OOP principles, namely **classes**, **objects**, **inheritance**, **polymorphism**, **encapsulation**, and **abstraction**. These may sound intimidating at first, but through hands-on implementation, you'll soon see how these ideas come together to simplify complex problems. To bring these concepts to life, we will construct a **console-based Library Management System**. This system will allow users to manage a collection of books, register library members, and perform lending transactions.

By building this system step-by-step, you will not only gain deep insight into Java's object-oriented design but also begin to develop the software architecture skills required to scale and evolve real-world applications.

Understanding Classes and Objects

To begin with, a **class** is a blueprint — it defines what an object should contain and how it should behave. It includes variables (called fields or attributes) and methods (functions that operate on the fields). An **object** is an actual instance of a class; it's a representation of a real-world entity like a `Book`, a `Member`, or a `Library`.

Let us consider the following class

```
public class Book {
    String title;
    String author;
    String isbn;
    boolean isAvailable;

    public void borrow() {
        isAvailable = false;
    }

    public void returnBook() {
        isAvailable = true;
    }
}
```

Here, `Book` is a class. When we create an object of this class using `new Book()`, we are constructing a real book in memory.

Visually, this relationship can be represented as

The concept of objects mirrors real life. A class defines the "type of thing" and each object is a specific instance of that thing.

Inheritance and Polymorphism Building

Inheritance allows one class to derive properties and behavior from another. This promotes code reuse and hierarchical classification. For instance, consider two types of library users Student and Teacher. Both are Members of the library, but they might have different borrowing limits.

We can define a base class `Member` and then extend it

```java
public class Member {
    String name;
    int id;

    public void borrowBook(Book book) {
        // default behavior
    }
}

public class Student extends Member {
    int borrowingLimit = 3;
}

public class Teacher extends Member {
    int borrowingLimit = 10;
}
```

This creates a clear hierarchy

```
        Member
      /        \
  Student      Teacher
```

Polymorphism means "many forms." With inheritance, it allows us to treat different derived objects uniformly. For example, both `Student` and `Teacher` can be used where a `Member` is expected

```java
public void registerMember(Member m) {
    // works for Student or Teacher
}
```

This makes your system more flexible and extensible — new member types can be added without changing existing code.

Abstraction Designing Clean Interfaces

Encapsulation is about hiding internal state and exposing only what is necessary. In Java, this is done using `private` fields and `public` getter/setter methods

```java
public class Book {
    private String title;
    private boolean isAvailable;

    public String getTitle() {
        return title;
    }

    public boolean isAvailable() {
        return isAvailable;
    }

    public void borrow() {
        if (isAvailable) isAvailable = false;
    }
}
```

This prevents misuse of internal fields and keeps data safe from unintended interference.

Abstraction means designing classes and interfaces in a way that the complexity is hidden from the user. For example, a `Library` class may internally manage a list of books, but expose only simple methods like `addBook`, `issueBook`, or `searchBook`. The user doesn't need to know how the books are stored or retrieved.

Building the Library Management System — Hands-On Project

Let's now implement a simple yet fully functional **Library Management System** in Java, leveraging all the OOP principles.

Project Structure

We will have the following classes

1. `Book` – Represents each book in the library.
2. `Member` – A base class for users of the library.
3. `Student` and `Teacher` – Subclasses of `Member`.
4. `Transaction` – Represents borrowing or returning events.
5. `Library` – Manages books and members.

Step-by-Step Implementation

Let's begin by coding the `Book` class

```
public class Book {
    private String title;
    private String author;
    private String isbn;
    private boolean isAvailable = true;
```

32

```java
    public Book(String title, String author, String
isbn) {
        this.title = title;
        this.author = author;
        this.isbn = isbn;
    }

    public boolean isAvailable() {
        return isAvailable;
    }

    public void borrow() {
        isAvailable = false;
    }

    public void returnBook() {
        isAvailable = true;
    }

    public String getTitle() {
        return title;
    }
}
```

Then the Member hierarchy

```java
public abstract class Member {
    protected String name;
    protected int id;

    public Member(String name, int id) {
        this.name = name;
        this.id = id;
    }

    public abstract int getBorrowLimit();

    public String getName() {
        return name;
```

```
        }
}

public class Student extends Member {
    public Student(String name, int id) {
        super(name, id);
    }

    public int getBorrowLimit() {
        return 3;
    }
}

public class Teacher extends Member {
    public Teacher(String name, int id) {
        super(name, id);
    }

    public int getBorrowLimit() {
        return 10;
    }
}
```

Now let's define the Transaction

```
public class Transaction {
    private Member member;
    private Book book;
    private String type; // "borrow" or "return"

    public Transaction(Member member, Book book,
String type) {
        this.member = member;
        this.book = book;
        this.type = type;
    }

    public String getSummary() {
        return member.getName() + " " + type + "ed
book  " + book.getTitle();
```

```
    }
}
```

Finally, the `Library`

```
import java.util.*;

public class Library {
    private List<Book> books = new ArrayList<>();
    private List<Member> members = new ArrayList<>();
    private List<Transaction> transactions = new
ArrayList<>();

    public void addBook(Book book) {
        books.add(book);
    }

    public void addMember(Member member) {
        members.add(member);
    }

    public void borrowBook(Member member, String
title) {
        for (Book book    books) {
            if
(book.getTitle().equalsIgnoreCase(title) &&
book.isAvailable()) {
                book.borrow();
                transactions.add(new
Transaction(member, book, "borrow"));
                System.out.println(member.getName() +
" borrowed " + title);
                return;
            }
        }
        System.out.println("Book not available.");
    }

    public void returnBook(Member member, String
title) {
```

```java
        for (Book book   books) {
            if
(book.getTitle().equalsIgnoreCase(title) &&
!book.isAvailable()) {
                book.returnBook();
                transactions.add(new
Transaction(member, book, "return"));
                System.out.println(member.getName() +
" returned " + title);
                return;
            }
        }
        System.out.println("Invalid return
attempt.");
    }

    public void printTransactions() {
        for (Transaction t   transactions) {
            System.out.println(t.getSummary());
        }
    }
}
```

Main Program to Run the App

```java
public class LibraryApp {
    public static void main(String[] args) {
        Library library = new Library();

        library.addBook(new Book("Java 101", "James
Gosling", "1111"));
        library.addBook(new Book("OOP Concepts",
"Alan Kay", "2222"));

        Member alice = new Student("Alice", 1);
        Member bob = new Teacher("Bob", 2);

        library.addMember(alice);
        library.addMember(bob);

        library.borrowBook(alice, "Java 101");
```

```
library.returnBook(alice, "Java 101");
library.borrowBook(bob, "OOP Concepts");

library.printTransactions();
    }
}
```

This implementation demonstrates real-world modeling using object-oriented principles. Every concept discussed — encapsulation, inheritance, polymorphism, and abstraction — is actively applied in this project.

By building a working library system, you have taken a huge step toward understanding software design at a structural level. You've learned to model complex relationships using classes and objects, extend functionality using inheritance, treat different objects interchangeably through polymorphism, protect data using encapsulation, and reduce complexity using abstraction.

As your next challenge, you might try adding features like searching by author, checking member limits before lending, or even implementing a simple login system. This will deepen your understanding and help you evolve from just writing code to designing full-fledged applications.

In the next chapter, we'll bring our projects to life by adding **Graphical User Interfaces (GUIs)** using Java

Swing, and learn how to connect object-oriented backend logic with interactive frontends — bringing you even closer to real-world software development.

Chapter 4

GUI Programming with Java Swing – Building Interactive Applications from the Ground Up

Learning to build interactive graphical user interfaces (GUIs) is a crucial step for every aspiring Java programmer. Java Swing is one of the most accessible and widely-used frameworks for desktop GUI development, offering a robust set of tools for creating interactive applications that are both functional and user-friendly. In this chapter, readers will not only explore the fundamentals of Java Swing but also develop a fully functioning, file-based To-Do List application. This real-world project introduces components like JFrame, JButton, JTextField, and event handling mechanisms, solidifying core concepts through practical hands-on learning.

Introduction to Java Swing and Its GUI Components

Java Swing is a part of Java Foundation Classes (JFC), providing a rich set of components for building platform-independent GUIs. Unlike earlier AWT components, which were dependent on native system GUI elements, Swing components are written entirely in Java and rendered by the Java runtime, allowing for a consistent look across platforms.

At the heart of every Swing application lies a JFrame, the main window that houses other UI elements. Within a JFrame, developers can place components like buttons (JButton), text fields (JTextField), labels (JLabel), checkboxes (JCheckBox), and more. These

40

components are part of the `javax.swing` package, which needs to be imported at the beginning of every GUI application.

Here is a quick overview of the core components used in this chapter

Component	Purpose
JFrame	Serves as the main window of the application
JButton	Clickable button that triggers actions
JTextField	Allows the user to enter or display a single line of text
JLabel	Displays text labels in the window
JPanel	A container for grouping multiple components
JScrollPane	Adds scrolling capability to components

Component	Purpose
JList	Displays a list of items and supports selection

These components are organized using layout managers like FlowLayout, BorderLayout, or GridLayout to define how components are arranged within a container. For our To-Do List app, we will use BoxLayout for vertical arrangement and FlowLayout for forms.

Understanding Event Handling and Listeners in Swing

Event handling is at the core of GUI interactivity. In Swing, every component can generate events such as a mouse click or a text change, and the application must respond to these events accordingly. Java uses event listeners, which are interfaces that contain methods to handle specific types of events.

For example, to respond to a button click, you need to implement an ActionListener, which requires defining the actionPerformed() method. When the user clicks the button, this method is executed.

Here's a simple diagram showing how events flow in a Swing application

In our To-Do List application, we will use `ActionListener` for handling button clicks like "Add Task", "Delete Task", and "Save List".

Hands-On Project   Building a File-Based To-Do List Application with Swing

Let's now create a fully working desktop To-Do List application using Java Swing. This app will allow users to

1. Add tasks to a list
2. Remove selected tasks
3. Save the list to a text file
4. Load tasks from a text file at startup

Step-by-Step Development

To guide readers in mastering Swing GUI programming, we'll build the project in carefully structured steps, allowing learners to observe their progress as new features are added.

Step 1 Create the Main JFrame Window

We start by setting up the main window using JFrame.

```
import javax.swing.*;

public class TodoApp {
    public static void main(String[] args) {
        SwingUtilities.invokeLater(() -> new
TodoGUI().createAndShowGUI());
    }
}
```

The TodoGUI class will contain all GUI elements and logic.

Step 2 Designing the GUI Layout

We use `BoxLayout` and `JPanel` to organize elements vertically.

```
public class TodoGUI {
    private JFrame frame;
    private DefaultListModel<String> listModel;
    private JList<String> taskList;
    private JTextField taskField;

    public void createAndShowGUI() {
        frame = new JFrame("To-Do List");

frame.setDefaultCloseOperation(JFrame.EXIT_ON_CLOSE);
        frame.setSize(400, 400);

        JPanel panel = new JPanel();
        panel.setLayout(new BoxLayout(panel,
BoxLayout.Y_AXIS));

        taskField = new JTextField(20);
        JButton addButton = new JButton("Add Task");
        JButton removeButton = new JButton("Remove
Task");
        JButton saveButton = new JButton("Save
Tasks");

        listModel = new DefaultListModel<>();
        taskList = new JList<>(listModel);
        JScrollPane scrollPane = new
JScrollPane(taskList);

        addButton.addActionListener(e -> addTask());
        removeButton.addActionListener(e ->
removeTask());
        saveButton.addActionListener(e ->
saveTasksToFile());
```

```
    panel.add(taskField);
    panel.add(addButton);
    panel.add(removeButton);
    panel.add(scrollPane);
    panel.add(saveButton);

    frame.getContentPane().add(panel);
    frame.setVisible(true);

    loadTasksFromFile();
}
```

Step 3 Implementing Task Logic

We implement the core logic for adding, removing, and
saving tasks.

```
private void addTask() {
    String task = taskField.getText();
    if (!task.trim().isEmpty()) {
        listModel.addElement(task);
        taskField.setText("");
    }
}

private void removeTask() {
    int selectedIndex =
taskList.getSelectedIndex();
    if (selectedIndex != -1) {
        listModel.remove(selectedIndex);
    }
}

private void saveTasksToFile() {
    try (PrintWriter writer = new
PrintWriter("tasks.txt")) {
        for (int i = 0; i < listModel.size();
i++) {
```

```
writer.println(listModel.getElementAt(i));
            }
        } catch (IOException e) {
            JOptionPane.showMessageDialog(frame,
"Error saving tasks");
        }
    }

    private void loadTasksFromFile() {
        try (BufferedReader reader = new
BufferedReader(new FileReader("tasks.txt"))) {
            String line;
            while ((line = reader.readLine()) !=
null) {
                listModel.addElement(line);
            }
        } catch (IOException e) {
            // File might not exist yet, and that's
okay.
        }
    }
}
```

This final part of the code ensures that tasks are persistent. When users reopen the application, their tasks are reloaded from the previous session.

By developing a practical application from scratch, readers gain hands-on experience in structuring GUI components, handling user input, and managing persistent data using file I/O. This foundation enables learners to extend their app-building capabilities into more complex projects, such as password managers, note-taking applications, or even basic accounting software.

Moreover, they get introduced to the MVC (Model-View-Controller) pattern, even if not explicitly defined. The data model (`listModel`), view (`JFrame` and components), and controller (event handlers) are conceptually separated, helping readers transition into more professional software design practices.

As learners move forward, they are encouraged to enhance this application by adding features like due dates, categories, search functions, and even JSON-based file storage or SQLite integration for richer experiences. Swing remains a powerful tool for mastering the core ideas of GUI programming, and projects like this equip readers with the skills and confidence to bring their ideas to life through interactive, persistent desktop applications

Chapter 5

Data Structures & Collections with a Task Scheduler

Understanding data structures is a fundamental skill for every aspiring Java developer. In the real world, applications manage and manipulate large volumes of data. Whether it's processing to-do lists, managing schedules, or handling contacts in a phone book, data structures allow developers to organize, access, and modify this information efficiently. In this chapter, we focus on mastering the Java Collections Framework, a powerful set of tools built into Java to handle common data structure needs such as lists, sets, maps, and queues.

To reinforce learning through hands-on experience, we will design and build a console-based **Task Scheduler** application. This real-world project will use different collections to manage tasks based on date, priority, and status. Through this process, readers will not only understand how each collection works but will also appreciate why choosing the right data structure makes a huge difference in performance, flexibility, and code maintainability.

The Need for Data Structures in Software Development

Before diving into code, it is important to understand why data structures matter. When designing an application, how you store and retrieve information can affect everything from speed to scalability. For instance, if you're creating a calendar app, you'll want to retrieve tasks scheduled for a specific day quickly. You might use a `Map` for this. If you care about the order tasks were added or need to check for duplicates, a `List` or `Set` becomes more appropriate.

Let us examine the primary Java collection types we'll use in this project.

Collection Type	Interface	Characteristics	Use Case in Scheduler
List	`List`	Ordered, allows duplicates	Maintain ordered task entries
Set	`Set`	Unordered, no duplicates	Track unique tags or categories
Map	`Map`	Key-value pairs	Schedule tasks by date
Queue	`Queue`	FIFO (First-In-First-Out)	Process time-sensitive

Collection Type	Interface	Characteristics	Use Case in Scheduler
		ordering	tasks

Each of these interfaces has multiple implementations in the Java Collections Framework. For example, `ArrayList`, `HashSet`, `HashMap`, and `LinkedList` are commonly used classes.

Java Collections Framework A Closer Look

The Java Collections Framework (JCF) is a unified architecture for representing and manipulating collections. It reduces programming effort by providing useful data structures and algorithms that have been tested for performance and reliability.

Core Interfaces and Classes

The framework includes interfaces such as `Collection`, `List`, `Set`, `Map`, and `Queue`, and classes such as `ArrayList`, `LinkedList`, `HashSet`, `TreeSet`, `HashMap`, `LinkedHashMap`, and `PriorityQueue`.

Below is a simplified diagram that illustrates the hierarchy

52

Understanding this structure helps developers pick the right tool for their needs. For example, `ArrayList` is great for fast access via indexes, while `LinkedList` is better for frequent insertion/removal. `HashMap` is ideal for quick key-value lookups, and `TreeSet` keeps elements sorted.

Project Overview Task Scheduler App

To reinforce learning, we will now build a console-based Task Scheduler application. This application helps users plan daily activities, set deadlines, and organize tasks based on their priority and date. By applying data structures in context, readers will not only understand how to use collections but also develop the skill to identify the right data structure for each requirement.

Features of the Task Scheduler

The following core features will be implemented

1. Add a new task with title, date, and priority
2. View tasks scheduled for a specific date
3. View all tasks sorted by priority
4. Delete a task by title
5. Store tasks using a Map keyed by date, with Lists of tasks as values
6. Use PriorityQueue to sort urgent tasks
7. Use Set to track unique tags

Designing the Task Class

Let us first define a Task class that encapsulates all attributes of a task. This class will be the core data object in our collections.

```
import java.time.LocalDate;

public class Task {
    private String title;
    private LocalDate date;
    private int priority; // 1 - High, 2 - Medium, 3
- Low
    private String tag;

    public Task(String title, LocalDate date, int
priority, String tag) {
        this.title = title;
```

```
        this.date = date;
        this.priority = priority;
        this.tag = tag;
    }

    public LocalDate getDate() { return date; }
    public int getPriority() { return priority; }
    public String getTitle() { return title; }
    public String getTag() { return tag; }

    @Override
    public String toString() {
        return "[" + date + "] " + title + "
(Priority  " + priority + ", Tag  " + tag + ")";
    }
}
```

Using a `Map<LocalDate, List<Task>>` to Organize Tasks

To retrieve tasks by date, we will use a `HashMap` where each key is a date and the value is a list of tasks on that date.

```
Map<LocalDate, List<Task>> schedule = new
HashMap<>();
```

When a new task is added, the system checks if the date key exists. If not, it creates a new list and then appends the task.

```
public void addTask(Task task) {
    schedule.computeIfAbsent(task.getDate(), k -> new
ArrayList<>()).add(task);
}
```

Using `PriorityQueue` for Urgent Task Sorting

To view the most urgent tasks first, we will use a PriorityQueue. This queue orders tasks based on priority.

```
PriorityQueue<Task> priorityQueue = new
PriorityQueue<>(
    Comparator.comparingInt(Task  getPriority)
);
```

Tasks with priority 1 (high) will be retrieved before those with 2 or 3.

```
public void loadPriorityQueue() {
    for (List<Task> tasks    schedule.values()) {
        priorityQueue.addAll(tasks);
    }
}

public void printUrgentTasks() {
    while (!priorityQueue.isEmpty()) {
        System.out.println(priorityQueue.poll());
    }
}
```

Using set to Track Unique Tags

We use a set to ensure that task tags (like "Work", "Health", or "Personal") remain unique and are not duplicated in the system.

```
Set<String> tags = new HashSet<>();

public void addTag(String tag) {
    tags.add(tag);
}
```

This can help in future enhancements where tasks can be filtered by tag.

Sample Console Interaction

The application can be extended with a simple text-based menu for user interaction.

```
Welcome to Daily Task Scheduler
1. Add Task
2. View Tasks for Date
3. View Urgent Tasks
4. Delete Task
5. Exit
```

Each action can call methods on the TaskScheduler class to modify or view the internal data.

Real-World Programming with Collections

Through this project, readers accomplish the following

Master the Java Collections Framework by using Lists, Maps, Sets, and Queues in a meaningful way.

Design data-driven applications where structure and organization are crucial.

Improve coding discipline by organizing logic into clean, modular methods and classes.

Practice problem-solving skills with real-world constraints like duplicate handling, priority sorting, and search by key.

Lay the groundwork for advanced systems like calendar apps, CRM tools, and task automation platforms.

By completing the Task Scheduler project, learners not only become proficient with Java collections but also take a major step toward becoming capable software developers. They move beyond theoretical understanding and begin crafting systems that manage data just like professional software used in the real world.

In future chapters, this project can be extended into a GUI-based calendar or integrated with databases for persistent storage, turning a simple console app into a fully-featured productivity tool.

Chapter 6

File I/O with a Note-Taking App

As aspiring developers move beyond console-based programs and venture into real-world applications, one of the most essential skills they must acquire is file input and output (File I/O). File I/O allows programs to persist data between sessions. Whether it's storing user settings, saving documents, or managing a library of information, file handling ensures that data created by the user or system is not lost when the application is closed.

In this chapter, we will embark on a hands-on project that serves a dual purpose to solidify your understanding of Java File I/O mechanisms and to give you the skills necessary to build a fully functional **desktop-based Note-Taking App** with features like creating, saving, and loading notes. This project will also help you work with different types of file formats including plain text (`.txt`), comma-separated values (`.csv`), and JavaScript Object Notation (`.json`). These formats are commonly used in various software systems for data storage and exchange.

Introduction to File I/O in Java

Java provides a powerful and flexible set of APIs for file handling through its `java.io`, `java.nio.file`, and `java.util` packages. Developers can use classes like `FileReader`, `BufferedReader`, `FileWriter`, `BufferedWriter`, `PrintWriter`, and more to read and write text efficiently.

Moreover, structured data formats like CSV and JSON are supported through additional libraries like OpenCSV and org.json.

The fundamental operations for File I/O can be grouped as follows

Operation	Java Class/Method	Description
Reading text	FileReader, BufferedReader	Reads characters or lines from a file
Writing text	FileWriter, BufferedWriter	Writes characters or lines to a file
Reading CSV	Scanner, String.split()	Parses lines of comma-separated values
Writing CSV	PrintWriter	Writes structured CSV lines
Reading JSON	org.json.JSONObject	Parses a JSON file into objects

Operation	Java Class/Method	Description
Writing JSON	FileWriter + JSONObject	Writes key-value data to a JSON file
Exception Handling	try-catch-finally	Ensures files are closed and errors are managed

Let us now move toward building our practical application that demonstrates all these concepts.

Note-Taking App with File Persistence

The Note-Taking App will be a simple desktop tool that allows users to write, save, and load notes. Each note can have a title, a body of content, a timestamp, and optional tags. The app will allow users to save notes in different file formats `.txt`, `.csv`, and `.json`. This ensures a hands-on experience with varied data serialization techniques and file operations.

Key Features of the App

To ensure clarity and usability, the app will offer the following features

- Create a new note with title and content
- Save the note in .txt, .csv, and .json formats
- Load a previously saved note from any of the supported formats
- Display all saved notes in a session
- Handle file-related exceptions gracefully

Designing the Note Class

The heart of this project is the Note class, which encapsulates all attributes of a note. Each note will be treated as a Java object which can then be serialized into various formats.

```java
import java.time.LocalDateTime;

public class Note {
    private String title;
    private String content;
    private LocalDateTime timestamp;
    private String tag;

    public Note(String title, String content, String tag) {
        this.title = title;
        this.content = content;
        this.timestamp = LocalDateTime.now();
        this.tag = tag;
    }

    public String getTitle() { return title; }
    public String getContent() { return content; }
    public LocalDateTime getTimestamp() { return timestamp; }
    public String getTag() { return tag; }
```

```
    @Override
    public String toString() {
        return "Title  " + title + "\nTag  " + tag +
"\nDate  " + timestamp + "\nContent \n" + content;
    }
}
```

Saving Notes as Plain Text (.txt)

For saving notes as plain text, we will write each
component of the note into a file using `BufferedWriter`.
The file will be named after the title of the note.

```
public void saveNoteAsText(Note note) throws
IOException {
    try (BufferedWriter writer = new
BufferedWriter(new FileWriter(note.getTitle() +
".txt"))) {
        writer.write("Title  " + note.getTitle() +
"\n");
        writer.write("Tag  " + note.getTag() + "\n");
        writer.write("Date  " +
note.getTimestamp().toString() + "\n");
        writer.write("Content \n" +
note.getContent());
    }
}
```

Reading the file back can be done line by line using
`BufferedReader`.

Saving Notes as CSV (.csv)

A CSV file is a compact and widely used format for
storing tabular data. Each note is stored in a line with

its attributes separated by commas. This is ideal for exporting data that might be used in Excel or spreadsheets.

```java
public void saveNoteAsCSV(Note note) throws
IOException {
    try (PrintWriter writer = new PrintWriter(new
FileWriter("notes.csv", true))) {
        writer.println(note.getTitle() + "," +
note.getTag() + "," +
                        note.getTimestamp() + "," +
note.getContent().replace(",", " "));
    }
}
```

To read notes back from a CSV, each line is read and split using `String.split(",")`.

Saving Notes as JSON (.json)

JSON is a flexible and human-readable format that allows for structured data. We use libraries like `org.json.JSONObject` to serialize a `Note` object.

```java
import org.json.JSONObject;
```

```java
public void saveNoteAsJSON(Note note) throws
IOException {
    JSONObject json = new JSONObject();
    json.put("title", note.getTitle());
    json.put("tag", note.getTag());
    json.put("timestamp",
note.getTimestamp().toString());
    json.put("content", note.getContent());
```

```
    try (FileWriter file = new
FileWriter(note.getTitle() + ".json")) {
        file.write(json.toString(4)); // Pretty print
with 4-space indentation
    }
}
```

This structured format is ideal for storing and exchanging data across systems.

Exception Handling in File Operations

File operations are prone to errors such as missing files, permission issues, or unexpected format problems. Therefore, exception handling is a crucial part of file I/O.

The following pattern ensures robust handling

```
try {
    // File operation code
} catch (IOException e) {
    System.err.println("Error reading or writing file
" + e.getMessage());
} finally {
    // Optional cleanup
}
```

Using the try-with-resources syntax is even better because it automatically closes files.

Visual Representation File Formats Diagram

Below is a simple conceptual diagram showing how one note is saved in different formats.

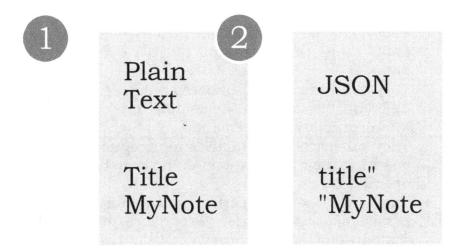

Building the Desktop Interface

If you've read the previous chapter on Swing, you can integrate the Note-Taking functionality into a simple GUI. Use a `JTextArea` for writing, a `JTextField` for title and tag input, and buttons for "Save as Text", "Save as CSV", and "Save as JSON". Upon clicking each button, the respective file saving method is triggered.

Skill-Building Outcomes for the Reader

By the end of this project, the reader will have accomplished several core milestones in Java programming

1. They will be capable of creating desktop-level applications that store and retrieve user-generated data.
2. They will have a deep understanding of how to use different file formats depending on context and interoperability requirements.
3. They will learn best practices in exception handling, ensuring their applications do not crash during file operations.
4. They will gain experience in integrating file persistence into the user experience of a software system, moving from ephemeral data to long-term storage.
5. They will be able to extend this project into a fully-featured application that syncs data with cloud storage or a database system.

The hands-on Note-Taking App project serves as an ideal sandbox to explore the power of Java file I/O. It combines logical thinking, attention to detail, and practical programming into one cohesive learning experience. Future enhancements could include search capabilities, encryption of notes, password protection, and data export tools, all of which will be easier to implement once the foundational understanding developed here is firmly in place.

Chapter 7

Multithreading with a Download Manager

As software applications grow more sophisticated, users increasingly expect speed, responsiveness, and the ability to perform multiple tasks simultaneously. Whether it's downloading multiple files, processing large datasets, or handling simultaneous user requests, the underlying principle that makes this possible is **multithreading**. In this chapter, readers will delve deep into Java's multithreading capabilities by building a practical, hands-on project a **Mini Download Manager**. This project will simulate multiple parallel file downloads, enabling the reader to understand core multithreading concepts such as `Thread`, `Runnable`, `ExecutorService`, synchronization, and concurrency control.

This chapter has been designed not only to enhance technical understanding but also to build real-world problem-solving skills through an end-to-end project that demonstrates Java's multithreading power. By the end of this chapter, readers will be able to confidently implement parallel processes in Java applications—an essential skill for any aspiring software engineer or hobbyist looking to build scalable applications.

Understanding Multithreading in Java

Multithreading allows a program to execute two or more threads concurrently. A **thread** is a lightweight subprocess, the smallest unit of processing. Java provides built-in support for multithreading, allowing developers to perform multiple operations at the same time, such as processing user input, updating the UI, and downloading files—without blocking each other.

The primary classes and interfaces involved in Java multithreading include

Feature	Purpose
Thread	Represents a thread of execution
Runnable	Functional interface representing a task that can run in a thread
ExecutorService	High-level API for managing pools of threads
synchronized	Keyword used to control access to shared resources
Future	Represents the result of an asynchronous computation

Feature	Purpose
`Callable`	Similar to `Runnable` but can return a result or throw an exception

Let us now explore how these elements work together through our main hands-on project in this chapter.

Project Overview Building a Mini Download Manager

The goal of this project is to simulate the downloading of multiple files in parallel using threads. While this project won't actually download files from the internet, it will mimic real downloads using sleep timers and progress updates. This simulation will be sufficient for mastering the principles of multithreading, thread coordination, synchronization, and managing shared resources.

Project Requirements

Each download will be treated as a separate task running in its own thread. A download task will print progress updates (like 10%, 20%, 30%...100%) to the console, sleep between updates to simulate time taken, and will be managed either using raw threads or a thread pool via `ExecutorService`.

Designing the DownloadTask Class

The `DownloadTask` class will implement the `Runnable` interface and simulate file downloading.

```
public class DownloadTask implements Runnable {
    private String fileName;

    public DownloadTask(String fileName) {
        this.fileName = fileName;
    }

    @Override
    public void run() {
        System.out.println("Started downloading   " +
fileName);
        for (int i = 1; i <= 10; i++) {
            try {
                Thread.sleep(500); // Simulate time
delay
                System.out.println("Downloading " +
fileName + "   " + (i * 10) + "%");
            } catch (InterruptedException e) {
                System.err.println("Download
interrupted   " + fileName);
            }
        }
        System.out.println("Completed downloading   "
+ fileName);
    }
}
```

Each instance of `DownloadTask` can be passed to a thread for concurrent execution.

Running Tasks Using Threads and ExecutorService

To simulate multiple downloads, we can use either individual threads or a thread pool using ExecutorService. A thread pool is generally more efficient and easier to manage.

Using Raw Threads

```
public class DownloadManager {
    public static void main(String[] args) {
        Thread t1 = new Thread(new
DownloadTask("file1.mp4"));
        Thread t2 = new Thread(new
DownloadTask("file2.zip"));
        Thread t3 = new Thread(new
DownloadTask("file3.pdf"));

        t1.start();
        t2.start();
        t3.start();
    }
}
```

Using ExecutorService (Preferred Method)

```
import java.util.concurrent.ExecutorService;
import java.util.concurrent.Executors;

public class DownloadManager {
    public static void main(String[] args) {
        ExecutorService executor =
Executors.newFixedThreadPool(3);

        executor.execute(new
DownloadTask("file1.mp4"));
        executor.execute(new
DownloadTask("file2.zip"));
        executor.execute(new
DownloadTask("file3.pdf"));
        executor.shutdown();
    }
```

```
}
```

Using `ExecutorService` ensures better performance when managing many concurrent tasks and allows greater control over task submission, execution, and completion.

Handling Concurrency and Shared Resources

When multiple threads interact with shared data (for example, updating a single file or counter), race conditions can occur. To prevent this, Java offers the `synchronized` keyword.

Let's say we want to keep track of how many files have finished downloading. We can use a shared counter with synchronized updates

```java
public class DownloadTracker {
    private int completed = 0;

    public synchronized void increment() {
        completed++;
        System.out.println("Total completed downloads
" + completed);
    }
}
```

Each thread will then call `increment()` after it finishes its download task.

Adding a GUI (Optional for Advanced Users)

For those who have already worked with Java Swing in previous chapters, this project can be extended with a simple GUI. Each file download can be represented by a progress bar (`JProgressBar`). When a `DownloadTask` is executed, it can update its associated progress bar in real-time using `SwingWorker` or thread-safe methods like `SwingUtilities.invokeLater()`.

This provides an engaging way to see multithreading in action visually and builds your practical software development skills.

Table Comparison of Key Java Multithreading Tools

Feature	Thread	Runnable	ExecutorService
Return value	No	No	Yes (via Callable/Future)
Reusability	Low	High	Very High
Performance	Slower with many threads	Efficient with pools	Optimized and scalable

Feature	Thread	Runnable	ExecutorService
Error handling	Manual	Manual	Better via Future/Timeouts

Real-World Relevance and Skill-Building

This project does more than teach syntax. It trains the reader to think in terms of processes, concurrency, and control. Many real-world systems use threads extensively—web servers handle multiple user requests via threads, background tasks in mobile apps run using thread pools, and high-frequency trading platforms rely on concurrency to process data in real-time.

By building this download manager simulation, the reader learns to

- Decompose tasks into units of parallel work.
- Use Java's concurrency tools to manage these tasks efficiently.
- Avoid pitfalls such as race conditions by using synchronization correctly.
- Create scalable applications by applying design principles like thread pooling.

In this chapter, the reader has taken a significant leap into advanced Java programming by exploring multithreading through a concrete, realistic project. The concepts of thread creation, task management using `Runnable` and `ExecutorService`, and concurrency control using synchronization form the backbone of high-performance software systems.

As you move forward, consider adding further functionality to the download manager implementing pause/resume capabilities, calculating estimated time remaining, handling real file downloads via HTTP libraries, and using `Callable` with `Future` to return download success/failure statuses. All of these build upon the strong foundation established here.

The skills developed in this chapter are essential not only for building your own multithreaded applications but also for understanding the performance architecture behind the tools and software you use every day.

Chapter 8

Networking with a Chat Application

In a world where communication is fundamental to both human interaction and software systems, the importance of networking cannot be overstated. Whether we are sending a message via WhatsApp, streaming a movie, browsing a website, or making a video call, networking plays a silent yet critical role behind the scenes. Java, being a platform-independent and powerful language, offers a robust set of tools to build network-based applications. This chapter is devoted to teaching networking principles in Java through the hands-on development of a **text-based chat application**, allowing multiple clients to connect and communicate in real-time via a server.

This project-centered approach will equip the reader with skills necessary to understand and implement core networking components like **sockets, TCP/IP communication**, **client-server models**, **port management**, and **real-time data exchange**. Through this process, readers will build not only a functional chatroom but also a strong foundation in how internet-based communication systems operate.

Introduction to Java Networking

Networking in Java is primarily facilitated through the **java.net** package, which provides classes and interfaces for implementing low-level networking features. At the core of Java's networking model are

sockets, which act as endpoints for sending and receiving data between devices over a network. There are two key types of sockets in Java `Socket` for client-side connections and `ServerSocket` for server-side connections.

Understanding how sockets work is crucial to building any networked system. A **server socket** listens on a specific port and waits for clients to initiate communication. Each client uses a **socket** to connect to the server, and once the connection is established, both ends can send and receive data. This communication typically happens over the **Transmission Control Protocol (TCP)**, which ensures reliable and ordered delivery of data packets.

Key Networking Components in Java

The table below outlines the essential Java classes used in building a chat-based network application

Class/Interface	Purpose
`Socket`	Represents the client-side of the connection

Class/Interface	Purpose
ServerSocket	Listens for incoming client connections on a specified port
InputStream	Reads data sent from the connected socket
OutputStream	Sends data to the connected socket
BufferedReader	Wraps InputStreamReader to efficiently read text
PrintWriter	Sends formatted text to the output stream
Thread	Handles each client connection concurrently in the server

Understanding TCP/IP and Ports

Before jumping into code, it's essential to grasp the basic concept of **TCP/IP**, which stands for

Transmission Control Protocol/Internet Protocol. This suite of protocols governs how data is exchanged over the internet.

TCP ensures that all packets of data arrive at their destination in order and without loss. IP handles the addressing and routing of these packets between devices. In the context of our chat application, TCP ensures that every message typed by a user reaches the server and is reliably relayed to other connected users.

Every connection in a networked application occurs over a **port**, which is essentially a numeric address on the device used to identify different processes or applications.

Building a Basic Multi-Client Chatroom

To fully understand how networking works in Java, we will construct a multi-client chat system. The system will have three main components

The Server Accepts incoming client connections, manages message distribution, and handles each client using a separate thread.

The Client Connects to the server, sends messages to it, and receives messages from the server.

Thread Management Each client connection is handled using a separate thread to allow multiple clients to interact concurrently.

Step 1 Creating the Server Program

The server listens for incoming client connections and then spawns a new thread for each client. All messages received from any client are broadcasted to all connected clients.

```java
import java.io.*;
import java.net.*;
import java.util.*;

public class ChatServer {
    private static Set<PrintWriter> clientWriters =
new HashSet<>();

    public static void main(String[] args) throws
IOException {
        ServerSocket serverSocket = new
ServerSocket(1234); // Port number
        System.out.println("Chat Server is
running...");

        while (true) {
            Socket clientSocket =
serverSocket.accept();
            System.out.println("New client
connected");
            new ClientHandler(clientSocket).start();
        }
    }

    private static class ClientHandler extends Thread
{
```

```java
        private Socket socket;
        private PrintWriter out;

        public ClientHandler(Socket socket) {
            this.socket = socket;
        }

        public void run() {
            try (
                BufferedReader in = new
BufferedReader(new
InputStreamReader(socket.getInputStream()));
            ) {
                out = new
PrintWriter(socket.getOutputStream(), true);
                synchronized (clientWriters) {
                    clientWriters.add(out);
                }

                String message;
                while ((message = in.readLine()) !=
null) {
                    System.out.println("Received  " +
message);
                    synchronized (clientWriters) {
                        for (PrintWriter writer
clientWriters) {
                            writer.println(message);
                        }
                    }
                }
            } catch (IOException e) {
                System.err.println("Error handling
client  " + e.getMessage());
            } finally {
                try {
                    socket.close();
                } catch (IOException e) {}
                synchronized (clientWriters) {
                    clientWriters.remove(out);
```

```
                }
              }
            }
          }
        }
```

Step 2 Creating the Client Program

Each client connects to the server, sends messages, and listens for incoming messages from the server using separate threads.

```java
import java.io.*;
import java.net.*;

public class ChatClient {
    public static void main(String[] args) throws
IOException {
        Socket socket = new Socket("localhost",
1234);
        System.out.println("Connected to chat
server.");

        new Thread(new
MessageReceiver(socket)).start();

        try (
            PrintWriter out = new
PrintWriter(socket.getOutputStream(), true);
            BufferedReader console = new
BufferedReader(new InputStreamReader(System.in));
        ) {
            String userInput;
            while ((userInput = console.readLine())
!= null) {
                out.println(userInput);
            }
        }
```

```
        }

    private static class MessageReceiver implements
Runnable {
        private Socket socket;

        public MessageReceiver(Socket socket) {
            this.socket = socket;
        }

        public void run() {
            try (
                BufferedReader in = new
BufferedReader(new
InputStreamReader(socket.getInputStream()));
            ) {
                String serverMessage;
                while ((serverMessage =
in.readLine()) != null) {
                    System.out.println("Message   " +
serverMessage);
                }
            } catch (IOException e) {
                System.err.println("Disconnected from
server.");
            }
        }
    }
}
```

Real-Time Communication and Threading

This chat application is a perfect example of real-time
data exchange using **multithreading** and **sockets**.
The server runs continuously and handles multiple
clients simultaneously using separate threads. Each
client runs a separate thread for receiving messages

from the server while still allowing the user to send messages via the main thread.

This concurrent execution model is central to real-time applications such as multiplayer games, video conferencing tools, and messaging apps.

Table Summary of Networking Terms Used

Concept	Definition
Socket	An endpoint for communication between two machines
ServerSocket	Used by the server to accept incoming client connections
Port	A logical access point for communication (e.g., port 1234 for our chat app)
TCP	Protocol that ensures reliable, ordered, and error-checked delivery
Thread	A lightweight subprocess used to handle

Concept	Definition
	each client independently

Hands-On Skill Development

By completing this chat application, readers gain real-world skills that are immediately applicable in many domains. Networking is fundamental to almost all distributed systems and applications. This project teaches

- How to establish and manage TCP/IP connections using Java.
- How to handle multiple clients with threading.
- How to design a scalable architecture for real-time communication.
- How to synchronize access to shared resources to prevent race conditions.

As a challenge, readers can take the project further by building a graphical user interface using JavaFX or Swing, implementing usernames and timestamps, or adding private messaging features. These enhancements not only test the reader's grasp of Java fundamentals but also help refine architectural and design skills crucial for professional development.

This chapter has guided the reader through the world of Java networking using one of the most powerful and illustrative applications possible a real-time multi-client chat system. Understanding and implementing this system provides a solid base in TCP/IP networking, socket programming, concurrency, and real-time data processing—all essential for building internet-connected applications, cloud services, and multiplayer systems.

By combining theory, code, and practical implementation, readers are empowered to take their Java skills to a whole new level and are now equipped to build their own real-world network-based applications with confidence.

Chapter 9

Databases with a Student Record System

In the modern software ecosystem, data is the most essential asset. Regardless of the type of application—whether it's an e-commerce platform, social network, or even a school management system—data persistence is necessary to ensure continuity, integrity, and utility. In this chapter, we will explore how to build a complete **Student Record Management System** using **Java Database Connectivity (JDBC)** and integrate it with a Graphical User Interface (GUI). Through this hands-on project, readers will learn how to connect Java applications to relational databases like **MySQL** or **PostgreSQL**, perform **CRUD operations** (Create, Read, Update, Delete), and build a full-fledged GUI application that interacts with the database.

This chapter not only focuses on the technical aspects of working with databases but also aims to elevate the reader's skill by helping them understand database design principles, SQL command execution, exception handling, and how to create user-friendly software for managing student records. By the end, readers will have built a desktop application that mirrors real-world systems used in educational institutions.

JDBC The Bridge Between Java and Databases

Java Database Connectivity, known as **JDBC**, is a standard Java API that allows Java programs to interact with relational databases. It provides a uniform interface for connecting to a wide variety of databases, executing SQL statements, and processing the results. JDBC forms the foundation of data-driven applications and acts as a translator between Java and the database.

To work with JDBC, the following components are involved

JDBC Component	Description
DriverManager	Manages the set of JDBC drivers and establishes connections
Connection	Represents a connection session with a database
Statement	Executes static SQL queries without parameters
PreparedStatement	Executes parameterized SQL queries securely

JDBC Component	Description
ResultSet	Stores the result of a query for processing

To use JDBC in your Java application, you must first include the database driver JAR file in your project. For MySQL, it is typically `mysql-connector-java.jar`, and for PostgreSQL, it's `postgresql-<version>.jar`.

Database Setup and Design

Before developing the application, we must set up a relational database. The following SQL command creates a `students` table, which will be used to store all relevant student data

```
CREATE TABLE students (
    id INT PRIMARY KEY AUTO_INCREMENT,
    name VARCHAR(100) NOT NULL,
    email VARCHAR(100) UNIQUE,
    course VARCHAR(100),
    grade CHAR(2)
);
```

This schema ensures that each student has a unique identifier, a name, an email address, a course, and a grade. The AUTO_INCREMENT keyword allows the database

94

to automatically generate a unique ID for each new student entry.

Connecting Java to the Database Using JDBC

The process of connecting Java to MySQL using JDBC follows these steps

1. Load the JDBC driver.
2. Establish a connection using a URL, username, and password.
3. Execute SQL queries via statements or prepared statements.
4. Handle the results using `ResultSet`.

Here is a simple Java class for connecting to a MySQL database

```java
import java.sql.*;

public class DBConnection {
    private static final String URL = "jdbc mysql
//localhost 3306/school";
    private static final String USER = "root";
    private static final String PASSWORD =
"your_password";

    public static Connection getConnection() throws
SQLException {
        return DriverManager.getConnection(URL, USER,
PASSWORD);
    }
}
```

Performing CRUD Operations with Java

CRUD stands for Create, Read, Update, and Delete. These four fundamental operations allow applications to interact with a database to manipulate records effectively.

The table below outlines each operation and its purpose

Operation	SQL Statement Type	Function
Create	INSERT	Add a new student record to the database
Read	SELECT	Retrieve existing records from the database
Update	UPDATE	Modify existing student data
Delete	DELETE	Remove a student record from the database

Create Operation (Insert Student)

```java
public void insertStudent(String name, String email,
String course, String grade) {
    String sql = "INSERT INTO students (name, email,
course, grade) VALUES (?, ?, ?, ?)";

    try (Connection conn =
DBConnection.getConnection();
        PreparedStatement stmt =
conn.prepareStatement(sql)) {

        stmt.setString(1, name);
        stmt.setString(2, email);
        stmt.setString(3, course);
        stmt.setString(4, grade);
        stmt.executeUpdate();

        System.out.println("Student added
successfully.");
    } catch (SQLException e) {
        e.printStackTrace();
    }
}
```

Similar code structures can be used for reading, updating, and deleting records using SELECT, UPDATE, and DELETE statements respectively.

Developing the GUI Application

To provide a user-friendly interface, we will use **Java Swing**, a part of the Java Foundation Classes (JFC) that provides a rich set of GUI components. The goal is to build a desktop app where users can add new students, view all students, update existing records, and delete entries with ease.

GUI Implementation Example

Here is a simplified version of a Swing-based student form

```
import javax.swing.*;
import java.awt.*;
import java.awt.event.*;

public class StudentForm extends JFrame {
    private JTextField nameField, emailField,
courseField, gradeField;
    private JButton addButton;

    public StudentForm() {
        setTitle("Student Record System");
        setSize(400, 300);

setDefaultCloseOperation(JFrame.EXIT_ON_CLOSE);
        setLayout(new GridLayout(5, 2));

        nameField = new JTextField();
        emailField = new JTextField();
        courseField = new JTextField();
        gradeField = new JTextField();

        addButton = new JButton("Add Student");

        add(new JLabel("Name ")); add(nameField);
        add(new JLabel("Email ")); add(emailField);
        add(new JLabel("Course ")); add(courseField);
        add(new JLabel("Grade ")); add(gradeField);
        add(addButton);

        addButton.addActionListener(e -> {
```

```java
        String name = nameField.getText();
        String email = emailField.getText();
        String course = courseField.getText();
        String grade = gradeField.getText();

        insertStudent(name, email, course,
grade);
    });

    setVisible(true);
  }

  public void insertStudent(String name, String
email, String course, String grade) {
      // Call JDBC insert logic here
  }

  public static void main(String[] args) {
      new StudentForm();
  }
}
```

This form can be extended to include JTable for displaying students, JButtons for update and delete operations, and validation for user inputs.

Skill Development and Real-World Application

By building this student record system, readers gain multiple valuable skills

1. Understanding of database schema design and normalization.
2. Mastery over JDBC connections and SQL command execution in Java.

3. Ability to design and code GUI applications using Swing.
4. Knowledge of exception handling and data validation for production-ready software.
5. Experience in integrating backend and frontend logic for seamless user interaction.

As a challenge, readers can extend the application to include features like search filters, export to Excel or PDF, login authentication for admins, or even cloud database integration using JDBC with remote database servers.

This chapter has demystified the process of connecting Java applications to relational databases, performing robust CRUD operations, and creating a fully interactive GUI-based student record system. In the process, readers have not only built a working piece of software but also gained the kind of industry-relevant skills required for enterprise Java development.

By learning how to architect applications that interact with databases securely and efficiently, the reader takes a significant leap in their software engineering journey—equipped now to build systems ranging from simple record managers to scalable enterprise platforms.

Chapter 10

JavaFX for Modern UI Development

As software development continues to evolve, so does the expectation for clean, professional, and responsive user interfaces. JavaFX is Java's powerful modern UI toolkit designed to meet these expectations. It allows developers to build rich desktop applications with advanced graphics, smooth animations, custom styling using CSS, and an architecture that separates logic from design. JavaFX is considered the successor to Swing and provides a declarative, maintainable approach to developing user interfaces. In this chapter, we will fully explore JavaFX by recreating the To-Do list application we built in earlier chapters—but this time, with a polished, interactive, and modern user experience.

By engaging in this hands-on project, readers will gain practical expertise in layout design, FXML usage, scene transitions, styling with CSS, and applying animations. They will also learn how to use **Scene Builder**, a visual drag-and-drop tool for JavaFX development, making it easier to design user interfaces without hard-coding all layout details.

Understanding JavaFX and Scene Builder

JavaFX is a software platform that enables developers to create desktop applications and rich Internet applications (RIAs). It uses a hardware-accelerated graphics pipeline and includes built-in support for 2D and 3D graphics, media playback, and modern UI controls. JavaFX applications can be written entirely in Java, or designed using FXML, which is an XML-based language that defines UI components declaratively.

To simplify interface development, **Scene Builder** is provided by Gluon (formerly by Oracle). Scene Builder is a GUI tool that allows developers to visually design their JavaFX layouts by dragging and dropping components. Behind the scenes, it generates FXML files that can be loaded by the JavaFX runtime.

Here's how the core JavaFX architecture looks

The **Stage** is the main window, and within it, a **Scene** holds all the UI components such as buttons, labels, and layout containers like VBox, HBox, and GridPane.

JavaFX Layouts and Styling with CSS

JavaFX provides a rich collection of layout containers that automatically manage positioning and resizing of child nodes. Some of the most common layout containers include

Layout Type	Description
HBox	Arranges nodes in a single horizontal row
VBox	Arranges nodes in a single vertical column
GridPane	Arranges nodes in a grid of rows and columns
BorderPane	Splits scene into five areas top, bottom, left, right, center

Layout Type	Description
StackPane	Stacks nodes on top of each other
AnchorPane	Anchors nodes to the top, bottom, left, and right edges

Using layouts efficiently is essential for creating adaptive, scalable interfaces. For example, using VBox and HBox together can create form-like interfaces where labels and fields are aligned neatly.

JavaFX also supports full styling using **CSS (Cascading Style Sheets)**. Developers can use an external .css file to style components just like in web development. This brings immense power in terms of consistency and reusability of UI design.

Example CSS for styling buttons and text

```
.button {
    -fx-background-color  linear-gradient(to right,
#36d1dc, #5b86e5);
    -fx-text-fill  white;
    -fx-font-weight  bold;
    -fx-background-radius  20;
}
```

```
.label {
    -fx-font-size    14px;
    -fx-text-fill    #333;
}
```

You can attach a stylesheet to the scene with the following code

```
scene.getStylesheets().add(getClass().getResource("st
yles.css").toExternalForm());
```

This approach allows separation of presentation and logic, making the application more maintainable.

Creating the To-Do App in JavaFX

We will now recreate the To-Do application we previously built, using JavaFX for a modern, polished look. The app will allow users to add tasks, delete them, and mark tasks as complete with a checkbox. Each task will be shown as a row with a label, a checkbox, and a delete button.

```
|                        To-Do App                       |
+--------------------------------------------------------+
|  Task Input Field               [Add Task Button]      |
+--------------------------------------------------------+
|  [ ] Buy groceries              [Delete]               |
|  [x] Finish project             [Delete]               |
|  [ ] Call plumber               [Delete]               |
+--------------------------------------------------------+
```

Each task is displayed inside a custom container (like an HBox) that holds a CheckBox, a Label, and a Button.

106

Using FXML and Scene Builder

Using FXML and Scene Builder simplifies the UI design process. First, create a layout file called todo.fxml

```
<VBox fx controller="TodoController"
     xmlns fx="http //javafx.com/fxml"
     spacing="10" alignment="TOP_CENTER"
padding="20">
    <HBox spacing="10">
        <TextField fx id="taskInput"
promptText="Enter a task..." />
        <Button text="Add Task"
onAction="#handleAddTask" />
    </HBox>
    <VBox fx id="taskList" spacing="5" />
</VBox>
```

This structure defines a vertical layout with a task input field and a dynamically populated list of tasks. Scene Builder can generate this visually, and automatically link it to a Java controller class.

Controller Code (TodoController.java)

```
public class TodoController {
    @FXML private TextField taskInput;
    @FXML private VBox taskList;

    public void handleAddTask() {
        String taskText = taskInput.getText();
        if (!taskText.isEmpty()) {
            HBox taskRow = createTaskRow(taskText);
            taskList.getChildren().add(taskRow);
            taskInput.clear();
        }
```

```
        }

    private HBox createTaskRow(String taskText) {
        CheckBox checkBox = new CheckBox();
        Label taskLabel = new Label(taskText);
        Button deleteButton = new Button("Delete");

        deleteButton.setOnAction(e ->
taskList.getChildren().remove(taskRow));

        HBox taskRow = new HBox(10, checkBox,
taskLabel, deleteButton);
        taskRow.setAlignment(Pos.CENTER_LEFT);
        return taskRow;
    }
}
```

This code defines how new tasks are added and removed. The createTaskRow method constructs a single row dynamically every time the user inputs a task. You can extend this functionality to allow storing tasks in files or databases for persistence.

Adding Animation for a Modern Touch

JavaFX includes a package called javafx.animation that allows developers to create smooth transitions and animations. This can greatly improve the user experience by providing visual feedback for user actions.

To add a simple fade-in animation when a new task is added

```
FadeTransition fade = new
FadeTransition(Duration.millis(300), taskRow);
fade.setFromValue(0.0);
fade.setToValue(1.0);
fade.play();
```

This small addition can make your application feel more responsive and modern. Animations can also be used to signal task completion, deletion, or error messages.

Final Project Features and Learning Outcomes

By the time the reader completes this project, they will have created a fully-functional, visually appealing desktop application that can be used on Windows, Mac, or Linux. They will also understand

- How to structure an application using JavaFX and FXML.
- How to design professional-looking interfaces using Scene Builder.
- How to implement logic through controller classes.
- How to dynamically add, update, and delete UI elements.
- How to enhance usability with CSS and animations.

This To-Do application is more than just a task manager—it is a complete learning environment where foundational UI principles are brought to life. Readers are encouraged to expand this project by integrating database storage, user authentication, and theming support to mimic the architecture of professional productivity tools.

JavaFX provides everything a developer needs to create high-quality, visually stunning desktop applications. Through this chapter, readers have learned how to separate UI and logic using FXML, utilize Scene Builder for visual layout creation, style applications using CSS, and implement animations to improve user experience. The hands-on project of building a modern To-Do app demonstrates how powerful and elegant JavaFX can be, providing an ideal foundation for any real-world application that demands a professional touch.

In the next chapters, readers can continue to expand their JavaFX knowledge by incorporating data persistence, charting libraries, or even web integration, setting the stage for enterprise-level application development.

Chapter 11

APIs and JSON with a Weather App

In today's digital age, applications are constantly interconnected with external services and data sources via APIs (Application Programming Interfaces). APIs enable applications to interact with other systems, retrieve data, and perform actions on external platforms. One of the most common use cases of APIs in applications is to retrieve real-time data from the web. This chapter focuses on how to build a weather dashboard app that fetches live weather data from a public API, processes it, and displays it to the user.

We will start by understanding how to make HTTP requests in Java, then move on to parsing JSON responses, which is a widely used format for transferring data. Finally, we'll integrate this knowledge by building a complete weather dashboard application that fetches real-time weather data using an API and presents it in a user-friendly interface.

Understanding HTTP Requests and Responses

To build a weather application, you first need to retrieve data from a weather API. This involves making HTTP requests to the API endpoint, sending necessary parameters (such as city name or geographic coordinates), and receiving the response in the form of data.

In Java, there are several ways to make HTTP requests, such as using `HttpURLConnection`, which is a standard Java class for handling HTTP communication. For more complex and efficient HTTP calls, you can also use libraries like **Retrofit** and **OkHttp**. Let's first explore how to use these techniques to fetch data from a weather API.

HttpURLConnection

`HttpURLConnection` is the standard Java class that allows you to send HTTP requests and receive responses. The typical workflow involves creating a connection, sending a request, and reading the response. Here is a basic example of making a GET request to retrieve weather data

```java
import java.io.BufferedReader;
import java.io.InputStreamReader;
import java.net.HttpURLConnection;
import java.net.URL;

public class WeatherFetcher {
    private static final String API_URL = "http
//api.openweathermap.org/data/2.5/weather?q={city_nam
e}&appid={API_KEY}";

    public static void main(String[] args) {
        try {
            String cityName = "London"; // Replace
with any city
            String apiKey = "your_api_key_here"; //
Replace with your OpenWeatherMap API key
```

```java
            // Create URL with dynamic city name and
API key
            String urlString =
API_URL.replace("{city_name}",
cityName).replace("{API_KEY}", apiKey);
            URL url = new URL(urlString);

            // Open connection
            HttpURLConnection connection =
(HttpURLConnection) url.openConnection();
            connection.setRequestMethod("GET");

            // Read the response
            BufferedReader in = new
BufferedReader(new
InputStreamReader(connection.getInputStream()));
            String inputLine;
            StringBuilder content = new
StringBuilder();
            while ((inputLine = in.readLine()) !=
null) {
                content.append(inputLine);
            }

            // Close the connections
            in.close();
            connection.disconnect();

            // Print the response (this is JSON data)
            System.out.println(content.toString());
        } catch (Exception e) {
            e.printStackTrace();
        }
    }
}
```

This simple code snippet fetches weather data in JSON format from the OpenWeatherMap API, given a city name and an API key. The URL is dynamically constructed with the city name and API key, and the data is retrieved via an HTTP GET request.

Retrofit and OkHttp

While `HttpURLConnection` works fine for basic requests, it can get cumbersome for more complex API interactions, especially when dealing with headers, request bodies, and managing asynchronous calls. **Retrofit** and **OkHttp** are modern libraries that simplify HTTP requests.

OkHttp is a powerful HTTP client for making synchronous and asynchronous requests in Java. It handles requests and responses efficiently and is used by Retrofit internally.

Retrofit is a type-safe HTTP client for Java, which simplifies API interaction. It abstracts away a lot of the boilerplate code needed for managing HTTP requests, especially when working with REST APIs. Retrofit converts API responses directly into Java objects, which simplifies parsing the returned JSON.

Let's explore a Retrofit-based approach for fetching weather data

Add dependencies (Maven or Gradle) You need to add Retrofit and OkHttp dependencies to your project. In your `build.gradle` file, include the following

```
implementation 'com.squareup.retrofit2 retrofit
2.9.0'
implementation 'com.squareup.retrofit2 converter-gson
2.9.0'
implementation 'com.squareup.okhttp3 okhttp 4.9.0'
```

Create a model class for weather data Retrofit will map the JSON response into a Java object. For this, you need a model class that matches the JSON structure returned by the API.

```
public class WeatherResponse {
     private Main main;
     private String name;

     public Main getMain() {
           return main;
     }

     public String getName() {
           return name;
     }

     public class Main {
           private double temp;
           private double pressure;
           private double humidity;

           public double getTemp() {
           return temp;
           }

           public double getPressure() {
           return pressure;
```

```
        }

        public double getHumidity() {
        return humidity;
        }
    }
}
```

Create a Retrofit interface This interface defines the API call and the endpoint.

```
import retrofit2.Call;
import retrofit2.http.GET;
import retrofit2.http.Query;

public interface WeatherAPI {
    @GET("weather")
    Call<WeatherResponse> getWeather(@Query("q")
    String cityName, @Query("appid") String
    apiKey);
}
```

Set up Retrofit Retrofit needs to be initialized with a base URL, which is the root URL for the weather API.

```
import retrofit2.Retrofit;
import retrofit2.converter.gson.GsonConverterFactory;
import retrofit2.Call;
import retrofit2.Response;

public class WeatherFetcher {
    private static final String BASE_URL = "http
    //api.openweathermap.org/data/2.5/";

    public static void main(String[] args) {
        Retrofit retrofit = new
        Retrofit.Builder()
            .baseUrl(BASE_URL)
.addConverterFactory(GsonConverterFactory.create())
```

```java
    .build();

WeatherAPI weatherAPI =
retrofit.create(WeatherAPI.class);

Call<WeatherResponse> call =
weatherAPI.getWeather("London",
"your_api_key_here");

try {
Response<WeatherResponse> response =
call.execute();
if (response.isSuccessful()) {
    WeatherResponse weather =
    response.body();
    System.out.println("City  " +
    weather.getName());
    System.out.println("Temperature  "
    + weather.getMain().getTemp() +
    "°C");
    System.out.println("Pressure  " +
    weather.getMain().getPressure() + "
    hPa");
    System.out.println("Humidity  " +
    weather.getMain().getHumidity() +
    "%");
} else {
    System.out.println("Error  " +
    response.code());
}
} catch (Exception e) {
e.printStackTrace();
}
    }
}
```

With this code, you can easily fetch and parse weather data using Retrofit. The response is automatically converted from JSON to the `WeatherResponse` object, making it much easier to work with.

Parsing JSON Responses

JSON (JavaScript Object Notation) is the most common format for transmitting data between a server and a client in modern web services. Java has several libraries available for parsing JSON, including **Gson** and **Jackson**. Gson is widely used due to its simplicity and speed. When using Retrofit, Gson is typically used to convert JSON responses into Java objects.

In the example above, Gson was used via Retrofit's `GsonConverterFactory` to automatically map the JSON response to the `WeatherResponse` Java object. If you were parsing JSON manually, you could use Gson like this

```
import com.google.gson.Gson;

String jsonResponse = "{\"main\" {\"temp\"
288.55,\"pressure\" 1016,\"humidity\" 87},\"name\"
\"London\"}";

Gson gson = new Gson();
WeatherResponse weather = gson.fromJson(jsonResponse,
WeatherResponse.class);

System.out.println("City   " + weather.getName());
System.out.println("Temperature   " +
weather.getMain().getTemp() + "°C");
```

This simple approach allows you to parse complex JSON structures efficiently.

Creating a Weather Dashboard Application

Now that you understand how to fetch and parse weather data using APIs and JSON, let's build a simple weather dashboard application.

The weather app will have the following features

- A user can input the name of a city.
- The app will display the current temperature, humidity, and pressure of that city.

JavaFX Layout for the Weather Dashboard

We will use JavaFX to create the user interface for this app. The user will input the city name, and the app will display the weather information dynamically.

Create the FXML Layout (weather.fxml)

```
<VBox fx controller="WeatherController"
      xmlns fx="http //javafx.com/fxml"
      spacing="10" alignment="CENTER" padding="20">
   <TextField fx id="cityInput" promptText="Enter
city name" />
   <Button text="Get Weather"
onAction="#handleGetWeather" />
   <Label fx id="weatherInfo" />
</VBox>
```

Controller Code (`WeatherController.java`)

```java
public class WeatherController {
    @FXML private TextField cityInput;
    @FXML private Label weatherInfo;

    public void handleGetWeather() {
        String cityName = cityInput.getText();
        if (!cityName.isEmpty()) {
            fetchWeatherData(cityName);
        } else {
            weatherInfo.setText("Please enter a city
name.");
        }
    }

    private void fetchWeatherData(String
```

Chapter 12

Java for Embedded Systems (Raspberry Pi Project)

Embedded systems have become integral to various applications, from home automation to industrial control systems. The Raspberry Pi, a popular low-cost, compact single-board computer, has become a go-to platform for building embedded systems and prototypes. In this chapter, we will explore how to use Java to interface with the General Purpose Input/Output (GPIO) pins of the Raspberry Pi, allowing us to interact with sensors, LEDs, and other peripherals. We will also explore how to cross-compile and deploy Java applications to the Raspberry Pi, creating a mini home automation controller.

Understanding the Raspberry Pi and GPIO

The Raspberry Pi is a versatile device that can run a full operating system (typically a version of Linux) and allows you to connect various external hardware components through its GPIO pins. These pins can be used to send and receive signals, controlling things like LEDs, motors, or reading data from sensors.

Java, being a powerful and flexible language, allows you to interact with the GPIO pins of the Raspberry Pi. However, since Java does not natively support GPIO, you need a library that provides this functionality. **Pi4J** is one such library that facilitates easy interaction with the GPIO pins using Java.

Pi4J abstracts the complexities of interacting with GPIO, making it easier to control hardware like LEDs, motors, and sensors. In the next sections, we will dive into how to set up your Raspberry Pi to work with Pi4J and how to interface Java with hardware to create an automation controller.

Setting Up Pi4J for Raspberry Pi

Before you start coding, you need to ensure that the Pi4J library is correctly installed on your Raspberry Pi. Pi4J provides a Java API for GPIO interaction, allowing you to manage hardware components.

Here is a step-by-step guide to set up Pi4J on your Raspberry Pi

Install Java on Raspberry Pi

The Raspberry Pi typically comes with Java pre-installed, but it is always a good idea to make sure that the latest version of Java is installed. You can do so by running the following commands

```
sudo apt update
sudo apt install openjdk-11-jdk
```

Download Pi4J Library

You need to install the Pi4J library on your Raspberry Pi. You can do this by following these steps

Go to the Pi4J website and download the latest release.

Install Pi4J using the following commands

```
sudo apt install pi4j
```

Verify Installation

After installation, you can verify if Pi4J is properly set up by running a simple program to blink an LED. If the program runs successfully and blinks the LED, you can be confident that Pi4J is working correctly.

Interfacing Java with GPIO Using Pi4J

Once Pi4J is set up, you can use Java to control the GPIO pins of the Raspberry Pi. The library provides a simple API to configure pins as input or output, send signals, and read data from external sensors or devices.

Blinking an LED Using Pi4J

Let's begin by creating a simple project to blink an LED connected to a GPIO pin. This project will help you get familiar with the basic Pi4J API, including how to interact with the pins.

Hardware Setup

Connect an LED to GPIO pin 17 (physical pin 11 on the Pi).

Use a 330-ohm resistor in series with the LED to limit the current.

Connect the negative leg of the LED to the ground (GND) pin.

Java Code to Blink an LED

Here's the basic Java code to blink the LED using Pi4J

```java
import com.pi4j.io.gpio.GpioController;
import com.pi4j.io.gpio.GpioFactory;
import com.pi4j.io.gpio.GpioPinDigitalOutput;
import com.pi4j.io.gpio.PinState;
import com.pi4j.io.gpio.RaspiPin;

public class LedBlink {
    public static void main(String[] args) {
        // Create a GPIO controller
        final GpioController gpio =
GpioFactory.getInstance();

        // Provision a pin as an output pin
        final GpioPinDigitalOutput pin =
gpio.provisionDigitalOutputPin(RaspiPin.GPIO_17,
"LED", PinState.LOW);

        // Blink the LED
```

```java
        for (int i = 0; i < 10; i++) {
            pin.high();  // Turn LED on
            System.out.println("LED ON");
            try {
                Thread.sleep(1000);  // Wait for 1
second
            } catch (InterruptedException e) {
                e.printStackTrace();
            }

            pin.low();  // Turn LED off
            System.out.println("LED OFF");
            try {
                Thread.sleep(1000);  // Wait for 1
second
            } catch (InterruptedException e) {
                e.printStackTrace();
            }
        }

        // Shutdown the GPIO controller
        gpio.shutdown();
    }
}
```

Explanation

GpioController Manages the GPIO pins.

GpioPinDigitalOutput Represents an output pin that can either be high (on) or low (off).

RaspiPin.GPIO_17 Refers to GPIO pin 17 (physical pin 11).

Thread.sleep(1000) Pauses the program for one second to control the blink timing.

When you run this program, the LED will blink on and off every second for 10 iterations. This simple project introduces you to the basics of GPIO control using Pi4J.

Building a Mini Home Automation Controller

In this section, we will build a simple home automation system to control LEDs and read sensor data. This system will allow you to control an LED based on the input from a button or a sensor, simulating a home automation setup.

Components Needed

- Raspberry Pi
- Breadboard
- LEDs
- Resistors (220 ohms for LEDs)
- Pushbutton
- Sensors (e.g., PIR motion sensor or DHT11 temperature sensor)

Wiring Setup

LED and Button

Connect the LED to GPIO pin 17 (as done in the previous example).

Connect the button to GPIO pin 18.

Use a pull-down resistor for the button to ensure a stable state when the button is not pressed.

Sensor (e.g., PIR Motion Sensor)

Connect the PIR sensor's output to GPIO pin 27.

Connect the sensor's power and ground pins to the corresponding pins on the Raspberry Pi.

Java Code for Home Automation Controller

```java
import com.pi4j.io.gpio.*;

public class HomeAutomation {
    public static void main(String[] args) {
        // Create GPIO controller
        final GpioController gpio =
GpioFactory.getInstance();

        // Set up the LED as an output pin
        final GpioPinDigitalOutput led =
gpio.provisionDigitalOutputPin(RaspiPin.GPIO_17,
"LED", PinState.LOW);

        // Set up the button as an input pin with a
pull-down resistor
        final GpioPinDigitalInput button =
gpio.provisionDigitalInputPin(RaspiPin.GPIO_18,
"Button", PinPullResistance.PULL_DOWN);

        // Set up the PIR sensor as an input pin
        final GpioPinDigitalInput motionSensor =
gpio.provisionDigitalInputPin(RaspiPin.GPIO_27,
"Motion Sensor");

        // Continuously check for button press or
motion detection
        while (true) {
```

```java
            if (button.isHigh()) {
                led.high();  // Turn LED on when
button is pressed
                System.out.println("Button Pressed
LED ON");
            } else {
                led.low();  // Turn LED off when
button is not pressed
                System.out.println("Button Released
LED OFF");
            }

            if (motionSensor.isHigh()) {
                System.out.println("Motion
detected!");
                // Implement actions when motion is
detected
            }

            try {
                Thread.sleep(500);  // Delay before
next check
            } catch (InterruptedException e) {
                e.printStackTrace();
            }
        }
    }
}
```

Explanation

GpioPinDigitalInput This represents an input pin. The button and motion sensor are configured as input pins.

motionSensor.isHigh() Checks if motion is detected. If the motion sensor detects movement, the system will output a message.

button.isHigh()   Checks if the button is pressed to toggle the LED.

This mini automation controller allows you to interact with the physical world. It reads sensor data and performs actions, such as controlling an LED or reacting to motion.

Deploying Java Applications to Raspberry Pi

Once you've developed your Java application, you'll want to deploy it to the Raspberry Pi. Since the Raspberry Pi uses an ARM-based processor, you may need to cross-compile your Java application to run it on the Pi. This step ensures that your application works on the Raspberry Pi's architecture.

Cross-Compiling Java Applications

To cross-compile a Java application, you can use tools like **Maven** or **Gradle**. These tools help you package your Java project into a JAR file, which you can then transfer to the Raspberry Pi.

For example, using Maven, you can package your Java project into a JAR file using the following command

```bash
mvn clean package
```

Chapter 13

Testing & Debugging Techniques

In the world of software development, ensuring that your application works correctly and reliably is just as important as writing the code itself. Testing and debugging are two critical techniques that can help developers ensure their programs run as expected and perform efficiently. This chapter will cover the foundational tools and practices used for unit testing, logging, and debugging in Java development. By mastering these techniques, you will be able to identify errors early, improve the quality of your code, and ensure that your applications run smoothly in production environments.

Unit Testing with JUnit

Unit testing is the process of testing individual units or components of a program in isolation to ensure that they function as expected. In Java, one of the most widely used frameworks for unit testing is **JUnit**. JUnit is a powerful testing framework that allows developers to write repeatable tests for their code, making it easier to validate that the code behaves correctly and meets its requirements.

The core idea behind unit testing is to create small, focused tests that validate individual methods or classes, ensuring that they work in isolation from other parts of the system. Each test is typically independent and does not rely on external resources like databases or file systems, which helps identify bugs early in the development process.

Setting Up JUnit

To begin using JUnit in your Java project, you first need to add the JUnit dependency. If you are using **Maven**, you can include the following dependency in your pom.xml file

```
<dependency>
    <groupId>org.junit.jupiter</groupId>
    <artifactId>junit-jupiter-api</artifactId>
    <version>5.7.2</version>
    <scope>test</scope>
</dependency>
```

If you're using **Gradle**, add this line to your build.gradle file

```
testImplementation 'org.junit.jupiter junit-jupiter-api 5.7.2'
```

Once the dependency is included in your project, you can start writing tests.

Writing Unit Tests with JUnit

Let's consider a simple Calculator class with a method to add two numbers. We will write unit tests for this method using JUnit.

Calculator.java (The Class to be Tested)

```java
public class Calculator {
    public int add(int a, int b) {
        return a + b;
    }
}
```

CalculatorTest.java (Unit Test for the Calculator Class)

```java
import org.junit.jupiter.api.Test;
import static
org.junit.jupiter.api.Assertions.assertEquals;

public class CalculatorTest {

    @Test
    public void testAdd() {
        Calculator calculator = new Calculator();
        int result = calculator.add(2, 3);
        assertEquals(5, result, "The addition result
should be 5");
    }
}
```

In this example

- **@Test** This annotation marks the method as a test method.
- **assertEquals** This assertion checks that the expected result (5) matches the actual result returned by the add method.
- If the values do not match, JUnit will report a failure.

Running JUnit Tests

You can run JUnit tests using your IDE's built-in test runner or through the command line. If you are using Maven, you can run tests with the following command

```
mvn test
```

JUnit makes it easy to automate testing, ensuring that your code remains functional as you make changes and additions to it.

Logging with Log4j/SLF4J

Logging is an essential part of software development, especially for debugging and monitoring applications in production. **Log4j** and **SLF4J** are two of the most popular libraries used for logging in Java applications. These libraries allow you to record important information about the application's execution, such as runtime events, error messages, and debugging information.

Log4j Overview

Log4j is a flexible and configurable logging framework that allows developers to log messages at various levels of severity (e.g., INFO, DEBUG, ERROR). These messages can then be written to different destinations, such as a console, file, or a remote server.

136

To use Log4j, you first need to include it in your project. If you're using Maven, add this dependency in your pom.xml

```
<dependency>
    <groupId>org.apache.logging.log4j</groupId>
    <artifactId>log4j-api</artifactId>
    <version>2.14.1</version>
</dependency>
<dependency>
    <groupId>org.apache.logging.log4j</groupId>
    <artifactId>log4j-core</artifactId>
    <version>2.14.1</version>
</dependency>
```

For Gradle, use the following dependencies

```
implementation 'org.apache.logging.log4j log4j-api
2.14.1'
implementation 'org.apache.logging.log4j log4j-core
2.14.1'
```

Using Log4j for Logging

Once Log4j is set up, you can start logging messages in your Java classes. Here's an example of how to use it to log messages in a Calculator class

Calculator.java (With Logging)

```
import org.apache.logging.log4j.LogManager;
import org.apache.logging.log4j.Logger;

public class Calculator {
```

```
    private static final Logger logger =
LogManager.getLogger(Calculator.class);

    public int add(int a, int b) {
        logger.debug("Adding {} and {}", a, b);   //
Logs the input values
        int result = a + b;
        logger.info("Addition result  {}", result);
// Logs the result
        return result;
    }
}
```

Explanation

- `LogManager.getLogger(Calculator.class)` Creates a logger specific to the `Calculator` class.
- `logger.debug()` and `logger.info()` These methods log messages at different levels of severity.
- In this example, DEBUG logs the inputs to the `add` method, while INFO logs the result of the addition.

Configuring Log4j

Log4j can be configured via an XML or properties file, where you specify logging levels, formats, and appenders (e.g., where the logs are written). Here's a simple **log4j2.xml** configuration file

```
<?xml version="1.0" encoding="UTF-8"?>
<Configuration>
    <Appenders>
        <Console name="Console" target="SYSTEM_OUT">
```

```xml
            <PatternLayout pattern="%d{yyyy-MM-dd HH
mm ss} [%t] %-5level  %msg%n%throwable"/>
        </Console>
    </Appenders>
    <Loggers>
        <Root level="debug">
            <AppenderRef ref="Console"/>
        </Root>
    </Loggers>
</Configuration>
```

This configuration directs Log4j to print log messages to the console in a specific format. You can easily modify it to write logs to a file or send them to a remote server.

Debugging Tools and Practices

Debugging is the process of identifying and fixing issues or bugs in your program. In Java, several tools and techniques can help you debug your code efficiently. These tools allow you to step through your code, inspect variables, and catch runtime and logic errors.

Using IDE Debuggers

Most modern Integrated Development Environments (IDEs), such as IntelliJ IDEA and Eclipse, come with powerful debugging tools built in. These tools allow you to set breakpoints, step through code line by line, inspect the values of variables, and watch how the program flow changes at runtime.

To start debugging in your IDE, follow these steps

Set Breakpoints A breakpoint is a marker in your code that pauses execution when the program reaches it. Set breakpoints on lines where you suspect errors or want to inspect the program's state.

Run the Debugger Launch your program in debug mode. The debugger will pause at breakpoints, allowing you to inspect the current state of the program.

Step Through Code Use the step controls to execute code one line at a time, allowing you to closely observe the behavior of variables and flow.

Inspect Variables While paused at a breakpoint, you can hover over variables to see their current values, or you can open a variable inspection panel to monitor multiple values simultaneously.

Exception Handling for Debugging

In addition to using a debugger, Java provides robust exception handling mechanisms that allow you to catch and handle runtime errors. By using `try-catch` blocks effectively, you can manage expected errors and log or display useful error messages that aid in debugging.

Example of Exception Handling

```
try {
    // Code that may throw an exception
    int result = 10 / 0;
} catch (ArithmeticException e) {
    System.out.println("Error  Division by zero!");
    e.printStackTrace();  // Print stack trace for debugging
}
```

Using Logging for Debugging

As mentioned earlier, logging with tools like Log4j can be invaluable for debugging. By adding detailed logging statements throughout your code, you can track the program's flow and catch errors before they cause issues in production. Logging at different levels (e.g., DEBUG, INFO, ERROR) allows you to capture varying amounts of detail depending on the situation.

In this chapter, we explored the essential techniques for testing, logging, and debugging Java applications. Unit testing with JUnit allows you to verify the correctness of your code, ensuring that your methods behave as expected. Logging with Log4j enables you to track the execution flow and capture critical information about your application's performance. Lastly, debugging techniques, including the use of IDE

141

debuggers and exception handling, allow you to catch errors early and fix them efficiently.

By mastering these tools and techniques, you will not only improve the reliability of your code but also become a more proficient developer, able to diagnose and solve issues quickly and effectively. With hands-on practice and a deep understanding of these concepts, you will be well-equipped to tackle more complex projects and build more robust applications.

Chapter 14

Packaging & Deployment

In the world of software development, building and deploying applications is as crucial as writing the code itself. Once an application is complete, the next step is packaging it into a deployable format, ensuring it can run on different environments, and making it available for use by end-users. This chapter will delve into the packaging and deployment process, including building Java Archive (JAR) files, using tools like Maven and Gradle for dependency management, distributing desktop Java applications, and an introduction to native packaging tools such as JPackage. By the end of this chapter, you will be equipped with the knowledge to prepare and distribute your Java applications efficiently, while also learning about advanced packaging methods that integrate your Java applications with operating system-specific formats.

Building JARs The Foundation of Java Packaging

A **JAR (Java Archive)** file is the most common method of packaging Java applications. It is a compressed file that contains all the class files, resources (such as images and configuration files), and metadata that make up a Java application. The JAR format allows developers to bundle their applications into a single, portable file that can be distributed and executed on any platform that has a compatible Java Runtime Environment (JRE).

The process of creating a JAR file is straightforward. A JAR file can be created manually using the **jar command** in the terminal, or it can be automated as part of a build process using build tools like Maven or Gradle.

Creating a JAR with the Command Line

To create a JAR file manually from the command line, follow these steps

Compile Your Java Classes Before creating the JAR file, make sure your Java classes are compiled into `.class` files. You can use the `javac` command to compile the Java source code

```
javac MyApp.java
```

Create the JAR File Once your classes are compiled, use the `jar` command to create a JAR file. Here's an example

```
jar cf MyApp.jar MyApp.class
```

    `c` Create a new archive.

    `f` Specifies the output file name (in this case, `MyApp.jar`).

This command will create a JAR file containing the compiled `MyApp.class` file. However, if your application has multiple classes or external libraries, the command would need to include those as well.

Creating an Executable JAR

For Java applications, an executable JAR file is one that can be run directly with the `java -jar` command. To create an executable JAR, you need to specify the entry point of your application (i.e., the `main` method).

Specify the Main-Class In the JAR file, you need to define the `Main-Class` attribute in the manifest file to indicate which class contains the `main` method. Here's an example manifest file

```
Manifest-Version  1.0
Main-Class  com.example.MyApp
```

You can either create this file manually or let the build tool do it automatically.

Create the Executable JAR Use the following `jar` command to include the manifest file

```
jar cfm MyApp.jar Manifest.txt com/example/*.class
```

This creates an executable JAR that can be run with

```
java -jar MyApp.jar
```

Using Maven and Gradle for Dependency Management

146

When developing Java applications, especially those that involve multiple libraries or external dependencies, managing those dependencies becomes crucial. Tools like **Maven** and **Gradle** simplify the process by automating the downloading, management, and inclusion of libraries in your project.

Maven A Popular Build Tool

Maven is a powerful build tool used in Java development for dependency management and project build automation. It uses an XML configuration file called `pom.xml` (Project Object Model) to define project dependencies, build configurations, and other settings.

To include dependencies in your Maven project, you need to specify them in the `pom.xml` file. Here is an example

```
<dependencies>
    <dependency>
        <groupId>org.springframework</groupId>
        <artifactId>spring-core</artifactId>
        <version>5.3.8</version>
    </dependency>
</dependencies>
```

Maven will automatically download the specified dependencies from the Maven Central Repository and include them in your project when you run the build.

Building a JAR with Maven

To build a JAR file with Maven, you need to add the appropriate plugin in the `pom.xml`. The most common plugin for JAR creation is the **Maven JAR Plugin**.

Here is a basic configuration for building a JAR

```xml
<build>
    <plugins>
        <plugin>

<groupId>org.apache.maven.plugins</groupId>
            <artifactId>maven-jar-plugin</artifactId>
            <version>3.1.0</version>
            <configuration>
                <archive>
                    <manifestEntries>
                        <Main-
Class>com.example.MyApp</Main-Class>
                    </manifestEntries>
                </archive>
            </configuration>
        </plugin>
    </plugins>
</build>
```

You can then build the JAR file by running the following command

```
mvn clean package
```

This command will clean the project and package it into a JAR file, including all specified dependencies.

Gradle A Flexible Alternative

Gradle is another build tool for Java projects that provides more flexibility and control over the build process. It uses a Groovy-based DSL (domain-specific language) for configuration. The key advantage of Gradle over Maven is that it allows for more complex and customized build processes.

Here's how you would define a JAR task in Gradle to build a JAR file

```
apply plugin  'java'

jar {
    manifest {
        attributes(
            'Main-Class'  'com.example.MyApp'
        )
    }
}
```

To build the JAR file using Gradle, you would run

```
gradle build
```

Gradle is highly customizable and allows you to add more complex logic to your builds, making it suitable for both small and large projects.

Distributing Desktop Java Applications

149

Once your Java application is packaged into a JAR file, the next step is distribution. For desktop Java applications, this means making it easy for users to download, install, and run your application. While JAR files are portable, they do require a Java Runtime Environment (JRE) to run, which may not always be installed on the user's machine. Therefore, packaging your application for easy distribution is essential.

Distributing as a JAR File

The simplest method of distributing a Java desktop application is by providing users with a JAR file. This is often done through a website or software repository. However, this method assumes that users have Java installed on their machines, which may not always be the case.

Creating an Installer

For a more user-friendly experience, you can package your JAR file into an installer. Tools like **Inno Setup** (Windows) or **pkgbuild** (macOS) can be used to create installation packages. These installers can automatically install the JRE if it is not present and allow users to install the application with a few clicks.

Another popular tool for creating cross-platform installers is **Launch4j**, which allows you to wrap your

JAR file into a Windows executable (.exe) file, and it can also bundle a JRE for easy deployment.

Introduction to Native Packaging Tools JPackage

JPackage is a new tool introduced with JDK 14 that provides a way to package Java applications into native installers for various operating systems. JPackage allows developers to create platform-specific executables and installable packages for their Java applications.

With JPackage, you can create native installation packages for **Windows**, **macOS**, and **Linux** that include both your application and a bundled JRE. This eliminates the need for users to have Java installed on their systems, providing a seamless experience for end-users.

Using JPackage

To use JPackage, you first need to build a JAR file, which contains your application's code. Then, using the `jpackage` command, you can package it into a native installer.

For example, to create a native installer for Windows, you would run

```
jpackage --type exe --input target/ --name MyApp --
main-jar MyApp.jar --main-class com.example.MyApp
```

This command will create a Windows executable .exe file, which can be easily distributed to users.

- --type exe Specifies the type of package (in this case, a Windows executable).
- --input target/ Specifies the directory containing the compiled JAR files.
- --name MyApp Defines the name of the package.
- --main-jar MyApp.jar Specifies the main JAR file.
- --main-class com.example.MyApp Defines the entry point of the application.

JPackage can also generate macOS .pkg installers and Linux .rpm or .deb packages. The benefit of using JPackage is that it simplifies the deployment process by creating platform-specific packages that do not require the user to install Java separately.

In this chapter, we explored the various techniques and tools available for packaging and deploying Java applications. We began by learning how to create JAR files manually and with build tools like Maven and Gradle. These tools not only help with packaging, but also automate the process of managing dependencies. We also covered the distribution of desktop Java applications, from simple JAR distribution to using native packaging tools like JPackage for creating platform-specific installers. By mastering these packaging and deployment techniques, you will be able to take your Java applications and distribute them to users, ensuring they run smoothly across different environments and platforms. These skills are essential for making your Java projects ready for real-world use.

Chapter 15

Capstone Project – Build Your Own Personal Assistant App

As we reach the end of this book, it's time to put everything you have learned into practice. This chapter focuses on combining all the concepts you've explored throughout the book into one comprehensive project building your very own **Personal Assistant App**. This app will integrate a wide range of features including scheduling, reminders, file operations, and optionally, voice input. By working on this capstone project, you will reinforce your understanding of core concepts and develop the skills necessary to build real-world applications.

Overview of the Personal Assistant App

A personal assistant app is designed to simplify the user's daily tasks by automating various activities. These tasks can include setting reminders, managing schedules, performing file operations, and even responding to voice commands. The personal assistant you will build in this project will be a modular, extensible application that demonstrates your proficiency in Java programming and application design.

In this chapter, you will break down the process of building the personal assistant app into manageable steps. You will leverage everything you have learned about **JavaFX** for user interface development, **APIs** for fetching data, **databases** for storing information, and

155

Java libraries for performing operations such as file management, scheduling, and reminders.

Planning the Personal Assistant App

Before you begin coding, it's important to plan the structure of the app and define its core functionalities. The app will have the following key features

Scheduling and Reminders

The app will allow users to set and manage schedules.

Users can create, view, and edit reminders, which the app will trigger at the appropriate times.

File Operations

The app will enable users to perform file-related tasks like creating, reading, and writing files.

This could be useful for storing notes, to-do lists, or other personal information.

Voice Input (Optional)

Using a voice recognition library, the app can accept voice commands to set reminders or perform tasks hands-free.

User Interface

The app will feature an intuitive **JavaFX** user interface, with options to manage reminders, view schedules, and interact with the system.

The design will follow a **modular approach**, meaning each feature of the app will be a separate module that can be independently developed, tested, and maintained.

Step 1 Setting Up the Development Environment

Before diving into coding, make sure your development environment is set up. You will need

JDK (Java Development Kit) installed on your machine (preferably the latest version).

A **build tool** like **Maven** or **Gradle** to manage dependencies.

IDE An Integrated Development Environment like **IntelliJ IDEA** or **Eclipse** will make it easier to develop and test your application.

JavaFX libraries for building the graphical user interface (GUI).

Optional **Voice Recognition libraries** (such as **Google Speech API** or **CMU Sphinx**) if you want to include voice input functionality.

Once your environment is ready, you can start by creating a new project in your IDE. If you're using Maven or Gradle, include the necessary dependencies for JavaFX and any other libraries you'll need for features like voice input or file operations.

Step 2 Designing the Modular Architecture

The core of this app is its modular architecture. This approach ensures that the app is maintainable, scalable, and easy to extend. The app will consist of several modules, each responsible for a specific functionality. The main modules will be

Scheduler Module

This module will handle the creation, viewing, and editing of scheduled tasks and reminders.

It will interact with a **database** (like **SQLite** or **MySQL**) to store user schedules and reminders.

File Operations Module

This module will manage file operations such as reading, writing, and editing files.

It will allow users to save notes or other information in text files on their computer.

Voice Command Module (Optional)

This module will use a voice recognition library to process voice commands, allowing users to control the app with their voice.

It will interact with the Scheduler and File Operations modules to execute voice commands like "Set a reminder" or "Open my to-do list".

User Interface Module

This module will be responsible for building the app's graphical user interface using **JavaFX**.

It will allow users to interact with the app visually by providing buttons, input fields, and notifications.

Step 3 Implementing the Scheduler and Reminders

The **Scheduler** will be one of the central features of the personal assistant app. The goal is to create a system where users can schedule tasks, set reminders, and receive notifications.

Database Design

You will need a database to store information about the tasks and reminders. In the database, each reminder will have the following fields

ID (Primary Key)

Task Name

Task Description

Date and Time (When the task is due)

Status (e.g., Pending, Completed)

Creating the Reminder Interface

Use JavaFX to create forms for adding new reminders. For example, you can use **TextField** for task name and description, and a **DatePicker** to select the date.

Once a reminder is set, it should be saved in the database.

Reminder Notification

You will need to implement a system to check if any reminder is due. This can be done using a **Timer** in Java. The Timer will check the database periodically to see if any task is due and, if so, display a notification to the user.

Step 4 Implementing File Operations

The **File Operations** module allows users to manage their files directly through the app. These files can be anything from notes to lists, and they can be easily accessed, edited, or saved.

File Management

The app will have basic file management features, such as creating new files, reading from existing files, and writing data to files.

For simplicity, the files can be stored as **text files**. Each file could represent a note or a to-do list.

Interfacing with Java File I/O

Use Java's **File I/O** classes (like **FileReader**, **BufferedReader**, **FileWriter**, and **BufferedWriter**) to read and write data to text files.

The user can interact with these files via the app's interface, choosing to save their data or open an existing file.

Step 5 Adding Voice Command Functionality

Voice input can greatly enhance the usability of a personal assistant app. By integrating a **voice recognition** library, you can allow users to interact with the app using spoken commands.

Integrating Speech Recognition

Choose a voice recognition library such as **CMU Sphinx** or **Google Speech API**.

Implement voice command processing, where the app listens for commands like "Set a reminder" or "Open my notes".

Command Handling

Once the voice command is recognized, you can parse it to determine what action to take. For example, if the user says "Set a reminder for tomorrow at 9 AM", the app will parse the date and time and add the reminder to the database.

Step 6 Designing the User Interface with JavaFX

The **User Interface** of the personal assistant app is built using **JavaFX**. JavaFX allows you to create modern and interactive UIs with minimal effort. The user interface will be divided into several sections

Main Screen

The main screen will have buttons to access features like scheduling, file operations, and voice input.

You will use JavaFX **Buttons**, **Labels**, **TextFields**, and **DatePickers** to interact with the user.

Schedule Management

The user will be able to view a list of upcoming tasks or reminders.

Use a **TableView** to display reminders in a clean, tabular format.

File Management

A section where users can create new files, open existing files, and view file contents.

This can be done using **FileChooser** and **TextArea** controls in JavaFX.

Step 7 Putting It All Together

Now that you have built each module of the app, it's time to integrate them. This involves linking the UI with the backend logic (database, file operations, etc.) and making sure everything works together seamlessly.

Modular Design

Ensure that each module is independent and can be easily tested. The modular approach will allow you to isolate problems and debug them efficiently.

Testing

Test each feature individually before combining them. Test reminders to make sure they trigger notifications, verify file operations to ensure files are created and read correctly, and check voice commands to ensure they are recognized and processed properly.

User Experience

As you integrate all the features, pay attention to the user experience. Make sure that the app is intuitive and easy to use. For example, add buttons that are clearly labeled and design the interface in a way that makes navigation simple.

Building a personal assistant app as a capstone project is an excellent way to consolidate everything you've learned throughout this book. By combining concepts like JavaFX for the UI, database management for reminders, and voice input for added functionality, you're creating a fully-fledged application that you can be proud of. This project not only reinforces your technical skills but also gives you the opportunity to practice the

Appendices

The appendices in this book serve as a valuable reference to help you further deepen your understanding of Java, troubleshoot issues you might encounter during development, and provide tools and resources that can assist you in becoming a more proficient programmer. Additionally, this section offers further project ideas and links to useful GitHub repositories where you can explore more hands-on learning opportunities and expand your Java development skills.

A Java Keywords Reference

In this section, we will cover the essential **Java keywords** used throughout your programming journey. These keywords are reserved words in the Java language that have special meaning and cannot be used for variable names, method names, or class names. Understanding these keywords is critical because they define the structure, behavior, and flow of your program.

Here's an overview of the most common Java keywords

Keyword	Description
abstract	Defines an abstract class or method,

Keyword	Description
	which is meant to be subclassed or implemented.
assert	Used for debugging purposes, enabling assertions within the code.
boolean	Declares a variable of boolean type, which can hold `true` or `false`.
break	Exits a loop or switch statement prematurely.
byte	Defines a variable of type byte, a 8-bit signed integer.
case	Defines a branch in a `switch` statement.
catch	Defines a block of code to handle exceptions.

Keyword	Description
class	Declares a class. Classes are templates for creating objects.
const	Not used (reserved for future use in Java).
continue	Skips the current iteration of a loop and proceeds with the next iteration.
default	Specifies the default case in a `switch` statement, or default value in interfaces.
do	Defines the start of a `do-while` loop.
else	Defines an alternate block of code that executes if the `if` condition is false.
enum	Defines a set of named constants.
extends	Indicates that a class inherits properties and behaviors from a superclass.

Keyword	Description
final	Prevents modification of variables, methods, or classes.
finally	Defines a block of code that will always execute, whether or not an exception occurs.
float	Defines a variable of type float, a 32-bit floating point number.
for	Defines the start of a for loop.
goto	Not used (reserved for future use in Java).
if	Defines a conditional block of code.
implements	Indicates that a class implements an interface.
import	Imports classes or packages into the

Keyword	Description
	current file for use.
instanceof	Tests whether an object is an instance of a specific class or interface.
int	Defines a variable of type int, a 32-bit integer.
interface	Declares an interface, which is a contract for implementing classes.
long	Defines a variable of type long, a 64-bit integer.
native	Specifies that a method is implemented in a language other than Java (usually C or C++).
new	Creates new objects or arrays.

Keyword	Description
null	Represents a null reference, indicating no object or value.
package	Defines a namespace for organizing classes.
private	Specifies that a member (variable or method) is private and can only be accessed within its class.
protected	Specifies that a member is accessible within its package and by subclasses.
public	Specifies that a member is accessible from anywhere.
return	Exits from a method and optionally returns a value.
short	Defines a variable of type short, a 16-bit

Keyword	Description
	integer.
static	Indicates that a member (variable or method) belongs to the class, rather than instances of the class.
strictfp	Ensures that floating-point calculations are consistent across platforms.
super	Refers to the superclass of the current object.
switch	Defines a switch statement for branching based on the value of an expression.
synchronized	Ensures that a method or block of code is accessed by only one thread at a time.
this	Refers to the current instance of a class.

Keyword	Description
throw	Throws an exception manually.
throws	Declares the exceptions that a method might throw.
transient	Prevents serialization of a variable.
try	Defines the start of a try block for handling exceptions.
void	Specifies that a method does not return a value.
volatile	Indicates that a variable may be modified asynchronously by multiple threads.
while	Defines the start of a while loop.

This table only provides a high-level overview of Java keywords. You will encounter these keywords frequently while developing applications, and each keyword has its own role in the structure and functionality of the program. Understanding when and how to use them is fundamental to becoming proficient in Java.

B Troubleshooting Common Errors

When writing Java programs, errors are inevitable. Being able to troubleshoot and resolve these errors is an essential skill for any developer. In this section, we will cover some of the most common errors you may encounter and how to handle them effectively.

Syntax Errors

These are the most common and easy-to-fix errors. They occur when you have mistakes in the structure of your code, such as missing semicolons, unbalanced parentheses, or incorrect variable declarations.

Example

```
int x = 10
System.out.println(x);
```

The error here is the missing semicolon after the declaration of x. The correct code should be

```
int x = 10;
```

```
System.out.println(x);
```

NullPointerException

This error occurs when you attempt to use an object that has not been initialized (i.e., it is `null`).

Example

```
String str = null;
System.out.println(str.length());
```

To resolve this, ensure the object is initialized before using it, or check for `null` values before accessing object properties.

ArrayIndexOutOfBoundsException

This error happens when you try to access an index outside the bounds of an array.

Example

```
int[] arr = new int[5];
arr[10] = 25;
```

Here, accessing index `10` causes the error. The valid index range is `0` to `4` for a 5-element array. Ensure the index is within the valid range.

ClassNotFoundException

This error occurs when the Java Virtual Machine (JVM) cannot find the class you are trying to load. This could be due to incorrect classpath settings or missing dependencies.

Solution Verify that all required libraries are in the classpath and that the class name is spelled correctly.

C Recommended Tools & Resources

To become an effective Java developer, having the right tools and resources at your disposal is crucial. In this section, we will recommend some of the best tools and resources to help you along your programming journey.

IDEs (Integrated Development Environments)

IntelliJ IDEA One of the most popular Java IDEs, known for its ease of use and powerful features like code suggestions, refactoring tools, and support for many frameworks.

Eclipse A widely used IDE for Java development, with a variety of plugins available for additional functionality.

NetBeans A free, open-source IDE that is known for its simplicity and good support for JavaFX and web development.

Version Control

Git A distributed version control system used to track changes in source code. Git allows you to manage and collaborate on projects effectively. Learning Git is essential for every developer.

GitHub A platform to host and manage your code repositories. GitHub provides a social coding environment where developers can collaborate on open-source projects.

Java Documentation

Official Oracle Documentation The official Java documentation is a vital resource for understanding Java APIs, classes, and methods. It is essential for learning how different parts of Java work.

Stack Overflow A vast online community where developers share solutions to common problems and discuss technical issues.

D GitHub Repositories and Further Project Ideas

One of the best ways to reinforce your learning is to participate in real-world projects. GitHub is an excellent platform where you can find repositories to contribute to or explore project ideas to work on independently. Below, we'll share some notable GitHub repositories and provide ideas for further Java projects that will challenge you and help you grow your skills.

GitHub Repositories

Spring Framework The official repository for the Spring framework, one of the most popular Java frameworks for building enterprise-level applications.

Java Design Patterns This repository contains examples of common design patterns implemented in Java, providing practical insights into software design and architecture.

Java Algorithms A repository that contains implementations of popular algorithms in Java, which can help you improve your understanding of algorithms and data structures.

Further Project Ideas

Expense Tracker App Build an app that allows users to track their expenses, categorize them, and view monthly spending reports. This project will reinforce your skills in JavaFX for building GUIs, as well as file handling for storing user data.

Student Management System Create a system that allows teachers or administrators to manage student records, including their personal information, grades, and attendance. This project will help you gain experience with databases and CRUD operations in Java.

Chat Application Develop a simple chat application that allows users to send and receive messages in real-time. This project will give you exposure to socket programming and networking in Java.

These repositories and project ideas will not only expand your knowledge of Java but also give you hands-on experience that you can showcase in your portfolio.

By exploring the resources and tools listed above and engaging with the troubleshooting techniques, you will build a strong foundation in Java programming. Hands-on projects will give you the practical experience necessary to transition from a beginner to a proficient Java developer, capable of building real-world applications.

THE END